The MAILBOX®

The Education Center®

20-Minute Science

grades K-1

More than **150** of the best ideas and reproducibles from our popular Investigating Science series

Updated for today's teachers and classrooms!

- **Practical activities**
- **Easy-to-do experiments**
- **Meaningful practice pages**
- **Engaging student booklets**

- **Timesaving patterns**
- **Songs that teach**

Science in 20 minutes or less!

Managing Editor: Kelly Robertson

Editorial Team: Becky S. Andrews, Diane Badden, Kimberley Bruck, Karen A. Brudnak, Pam Crane, Chris Curry, Pierce Foster, Tazmen Hansen, Marsha Heim, Lori Z. Henry, Kitty Lowrance, Mark Rainey, Greg D. Rieves, Hope Rodgers-Medina, Rebecca Saunders, Donna K. Teal, Sharon M. Tresino, Zane Williard

www.themailbox.com

©2012 The Mailbox® Books
All rights reserved.
ISBN 978-1-61276-218-0

Printed in the United States
10 9 8 7 6 5 4 3 2 1

HPS240375

Table of Contents

Life Science

Physical Science

Earth Science

20-Minute Science • ©The Mailbox® Books • TEC61363

What's Inside

A Year's Worth of 20-Minute Science!

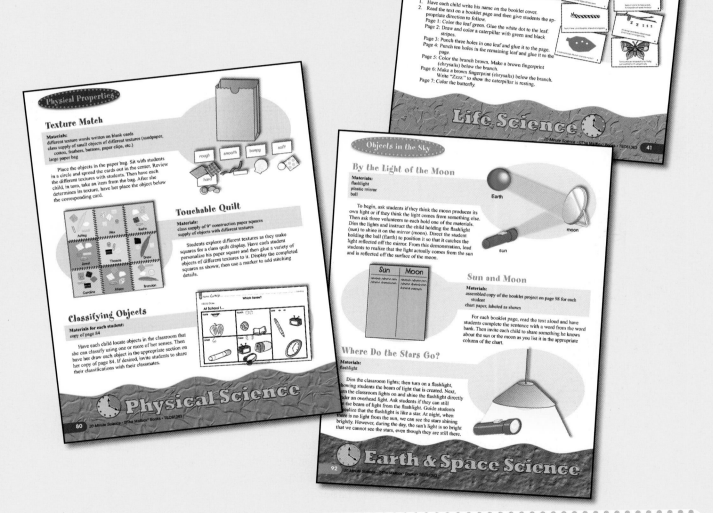

Timesaving Formats!

- Material lists
- Step-by-step directions
- Quick-to-read descriptions
- Helpful illustrations

Body-Part Pairs

Materials for each student:
blank paper

To begin, draw an outline of a head and torso on the board. Add a mouth and a nose. Then challenge students to name body parts that come in pairs. After a child names a pair, invite him to add the body parts to the drawing. Continue until all the pairs have been added. Finally, give each child a sheet of paper on which to draw a self-portrait, complete with all her body-part pairs.

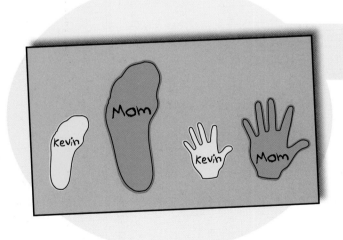

Big and Little Parts

Materials for each student:
9" x 12" sheet of construction paper
two 12" x 18" sheets of construction paper

Day 1: Explain to students that people have the same body parts, no matter if they're children or adults! Invite each child to have a partner help him trace his hand and foot (with his shoe removed) on a 9" x 12" sheet of construction paper. Then send home with each child a 12" x 18" sheet of construction paper with a note asking an adult family member or friend to trace her hand and foot on the paper and return it to school.

Day 2: Have each child write his name and the name of the adult on the appropriate tracings and then cut them out. Then have him glue the cutouts to the other 12" x 18" sheet of paper as shown. Guide students to realize that, even though the adult's body parts are bigger than theirs, they still look the same!

Life Science

Inside and Outside

Materials for each student:
assembled booklet project and patterns from pages 7–10
liquid glue

Discuss with students what we have covering the outside of our bodies as well as what is inside our bodies. Then guide students in the directions below to help them complete their booklets. Encourage youngsters to lift the flap on each page to reveal the body part that is inside!

Steps:
1. Cut out the patterns.
2. For each booklet page, put a small dot of glue on the black dot and place the corresponding pattern atop the glue.

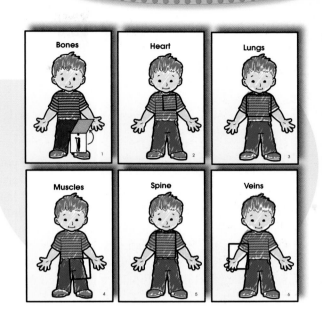

The Five Senses

Materials for each student:
copy of page 11

Have each child cut out the cards on her copy of page 11. Ask a volunteer to name a sense and tell which body part we use to experience the sense. Direct each student to glue that card in the appropriate box. Continue with each of the remaining senses. Then invite youngsters to pretend they are bakers like Bob on the reproducible. Invite each child, in turn, to name something he might see, hear, smell, taste, or touch in a bakery.

Life Science

"Sense-ational" Poem

Materials:
chart paper, labeled with the title, sentence starters, and
blank lines as shown

Call on youngsters to use their senses to help you create a sensory poem. To begin, ask students to brainstorm words that name things around the school as you list their responses on the board. Then direct students' attention to the chart paper and guide them to choose an item for each of the five senses. Have volunteers name a describing word for each item as you write the words in the appropriate blanks on the chart paper. Finally, read the completed poem together.

At School

I see <u>nice friends</u>.

I hear <u>the clock ticking</u>.

I smell <u>yummy cookies</u>.

I taste <u>delicious spaghetti</u>.

I feel <u>soft carpet</u>.

All at our school!

(sung to the tune of "Twinkle, Twinkle, Little Star")

Look at the [apple] I've found.	Point to eyes.
It is [red], and it feels [smooth].	Pretend to hold it.
The [sweet] smell is tempting me.	Pretend to smell it.
What a treat it will soon be!	
Next, I'll take a bite and hear	Pretend to take a bite.
A crunch, crunch sound in my ear.	Hold hand to ear.
It tastes good; here's how I know:	
My sense of taste has told me so.	Point to mouth.
All my senses, I used just now.	
Listen, and I'll tell you how!	Chant the senses.
Sight!	Point to eyes.
Touch!	Hold up hands.
Smell!	Point to nose.
Hearing!	Point to ears.
Taste!	Point to mouth.

Crunch! Munch!

Materials:
variety of crunchy snack foods (apple, carrots, crackers)

To begin, review the five senses with students. Then lead youngsters in this action song as a follow up activity. Display the apple as you sing the song the first time. Then sing the song again, displaying a different food and substituting appropriate words.

Life Science

1

Bones

Inside and
Outside
the Body

by _Dakota_

20-Minute Science • ©The Mailbox® Books • TEC61363

Booklet Pages 2 and 3

Use with "Inside and Outside" on page 5.

Lungs

3

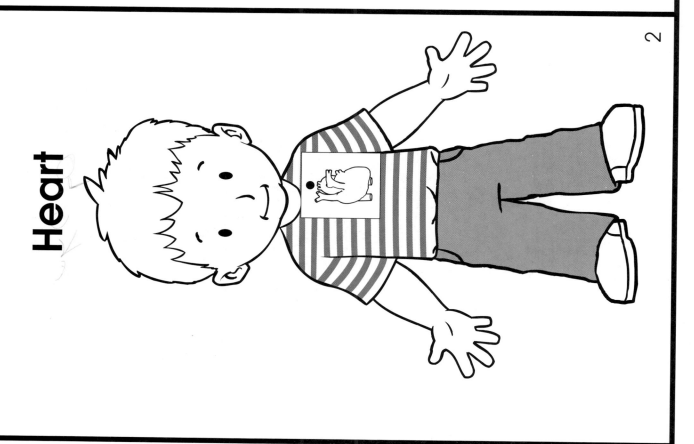

Heart

2

5

Spine

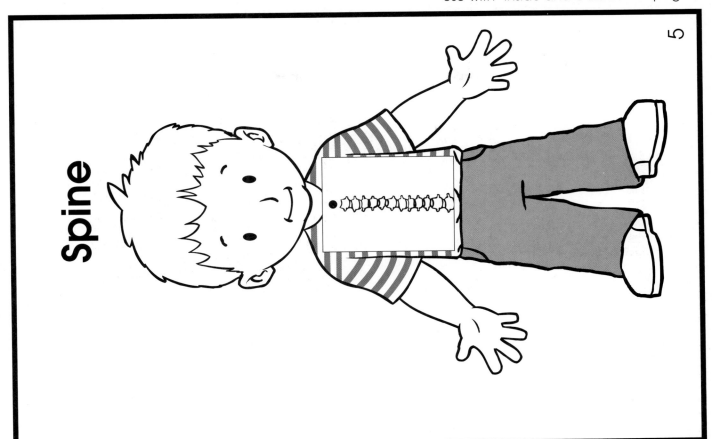

4

Muscles

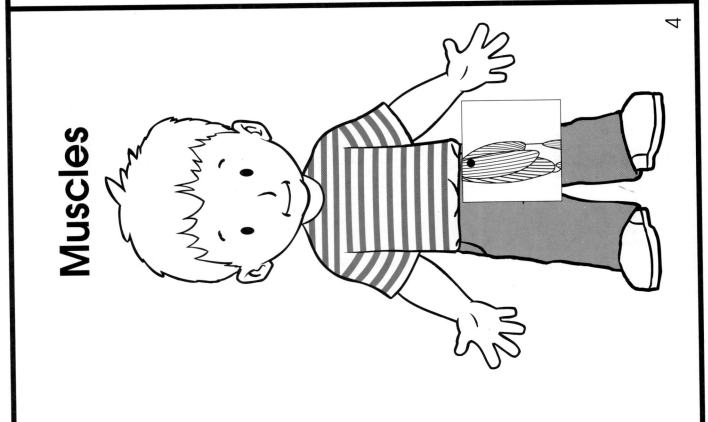

Booklet Page 6 and Patterns

Use with "Inside and Outside" on page 5.

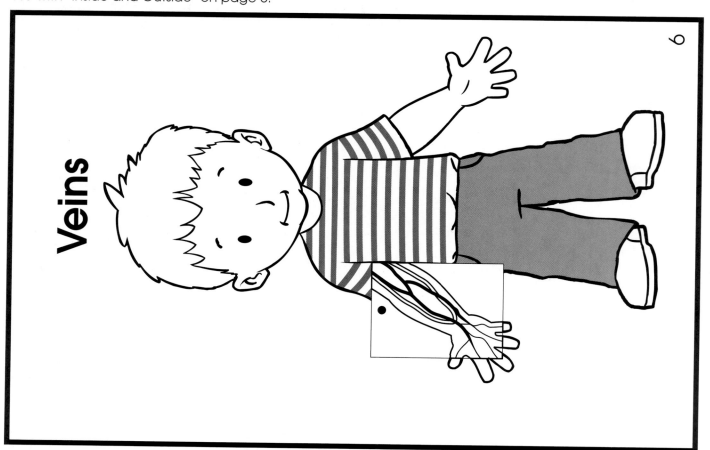

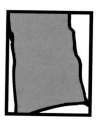

20-Minute Science • ©The Mailbox® Books • TEC61363

Name _____

Baker Bob's Five Senses

Cut.

Match.

Glue.

taste

touch

smell

hear

see

Identifying the five senses

20-Minute Science • ©The Mailbox® Books • TEC61363

Note to the teacher: Use with "The Five Senses" on page 5.

11

Animals

Which Kind of Animal?

Materials:
chart labeled as shown
magazines with animal pictures
tape

Day 1: Ask each student to cut an animal picture from a magazine. Then have each child, in turn, name his animal and tape the picture to the chart.

Day 2: Choose a category and ask students to tell how the animals are alike. Write their observation(s) on the chart. Repeat.

Mammals	Insects	Fish	Reptiles	Birds	Other
They have fur.	They have six legs.	It has fins.	They have scales.	It has feathers.	

Legs, Legs, Legs!

Materials for every three students:
copy of the animal cards on page 20
5 blank cards
scissors

Form groups of three students each. Have each group label its blank cards with the following numbers: 0, 2, 4, 6, and 8. Explain that the numbers tell how many legs an animal can have. Next, have each group cut apart its animal cards and sort the animals by number of legs.

Life Science

How Many Legs?

Materials for each student:
assembled copy of the booklet on pages 21–23

Have each student write her name on the cover of her booklet. Then, for each booklet page, instruct students to draw an animal with that number of legs, trace the number, and read the sentence.

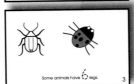

Basic Needs of Animals

Ask students whether they think an animal's basic needs are the same as a person's (food, water, air, and shelter). Then use this song to investigate the basic needs of animals.

(sung to the tune of "London Bridge")

Animals have basic needs,
Basic needs, basic needs.
Animals have basic needs
Just as we do!

A [robin] needs [worms to eat],
[Worms to eat, worms to eat].
A [robin] needs [worms to eat].
That's what it needs!

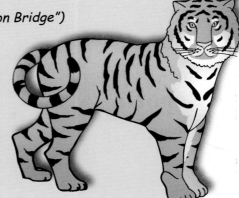

Continue, replacing the underlined words and phrases with different animal names and the animals' basic needs, such as *tiger, meat to eat,* and *lizard, air to breathe.*

Life Science

Growing and Changing

Materials:
student copies of page 24
baby picture of yourself

Show students your photo and ask them to guess who is pictured. Once you are named, invite students to describe the ways you have grown and changed. Explain that baby animals grow and change too. Then have each child complete a copy of page 24. Invite students to bring baby pictures of themselves to school so their classmates can see how they have also grown and changed.

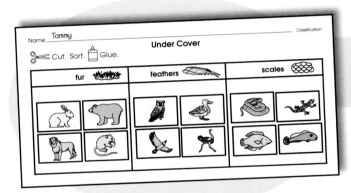

Animal Coverings

Materials:
pictures of animals with different coverings (fur/hair, scales, feathers, shell, quills)
student copies of page 25

Name an animal and show its picture. Help students identify the covering and determine how the covering helps the animal. Invite students to name additional animals with similar coverings. Repeat with each picture. Then have each child complete a copy of page 25.

Riddle Reports

Materials for each student:
copy of page 26
4" square of construction paper
tape

Day 1: Help each child tape a construction paper square where indicated on his copy of page 26 to make a flap. Then assist students as needed as they complete the activity.

Day 2: Invite students to share their reports with the class. Encourage classmates to guess the identity of each animal.

Life Science

What Mammals Need

Materials for each student:
sheet of manila paper

Steps:

1. Explain that mammals are animals that have hair or fur at some time during their lives. Also review the basic needs of animals (food, water, air, and shelter).
2. Ask students to name mammals. List their responses.
3. Near the list, write "My _____ needs _____ to live."
4. Have each student choose a mammal from the list, copy and complete the sentence with her mammal's name and one of its basic needs, and illustrate the mammal.
5. Compile the student pages into a class book titled "What Mammals Need."

Mammals

cat	mouse
dog	monkey
bear	fox
whale	horse
rabbit	tiger

"My _____ needs _____ to live."

Did You Know?
All mammals breathe air using lungs.

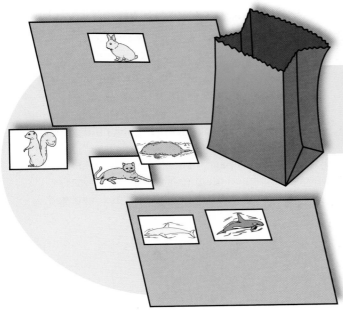

Land or Ocean?

Materials:
cards from a copy of page 27, cut apart
paper bag
blue sheet of construction paper
brown sheet of construction paper

Steps:

1. Name the animal on each card and help students understand why it is a mammal.
2. Put the cards in the bag. Put the bag near the sheets of construction paper.
3. Ask students where they think mammals live: on land or in the water.
4. Invite each student to take a turn removing a card from the bag and placing it on the brown paper for land or the blue paper for water.
5. Continue until all the cards are sorted.

Life Science

From Baby to Adult

Materials for each student:
copy of one card set from page 28
sheet of construction paper

Have each child cut apart her mammal cards and arrange them on her paper to show the growth sequence of a baby mammal. Then have her glue the cards in place and write a sentence that explains what the pictures show. Invite students with different card sets to compare their results.

This is a baby.

Home, Sweet Home

Materials for each student:
copy of page 29

Help students remember that mammals live on land and live in water. Then use this activity to show that mammals can live almost anywhere on Earth. Ask each student to point to a specific habitat (home) on his copy of page 29. Then guide students in naming mammals that live there. (See "Did You Know?" on this page.) Then ask each child to draw one of the named mammals on his paper in its habitat. Continue until each habitat is illustrated.

Did You Know?
Mammals live in lots of places!
Mountain habitat: bear, deer, sheep, goat
Ocean habitat: whale, walrus, dolphin, sea otter, seal
Desert habitat: camel, coyote, fox, jackrabbit
Forest habitat: raccoon, wolf, squirrel, rabbit, beaver
Grassland habitat: elephant, lion, zebra, rhinoceros, giraffe

Life Science

Bird Basics

Materials for each student:
copy of a card set from page 30
sheet of construction paper

During this activity, students discover that even though a bird's basic needs are the same as a human's, the basic needs of a bird look different. First, have each child divide her paper into two columns. Ask her to draw a bird at the top of one column and herself at the top of the other column. Then have her cut apart her card set, sort the cards on her paper, and glue them in place.

In the Nest

Spotlight the life cycle of a bird during this booklet activity.

Materials for each student:
assembled copy of the booklet on pages 31–33

Steps:

1. Have each child write her name on the booklet cover.
2. Read the text on a booklet page and then give students the appropriate direction to follow.
   Page 1: Draw lines to finish the nest.
   Page 2: Draw two more eggs in the nest.
   Page 3: Draw another cracked egg in the nest.
   Page 4: Draw a worm in the adult bird's beak.
   Page 5: Draw three feathered baby birds in the nest.
3. Suggest that students color their booklets and then use them to retell the story of a bird's life cycle.

Life Science

Fish Puppet

Students use this puppet to learn about the parts of a fish.

Materials for each student:
construction paper copy of page 34
jumbo craft stick
tape

Steps:

1. Have each child color and cut out a copy of the fish pattern from page 34.
2. Direct him to tape the craft stick to the back of his fish cutout.
3. Name a fish part. Ask each child to point to the part on his fish.
4. Help each child find that word card, cut it out, and glue it in the appropriate box.

Did You Know?
Fins help fish swim and balance.
Scales are slick and help fish glide through the water.
The tail helps push the fish through the water.
Fish use gills to breathe.

Fish Facts

Review several characteristics of fish with little ones. Then sing this song to help students learn what fish can do. If desired, have each child use her puppet from the idea above as she sings and performs the song.

(sung to the tune of "This Old Man")

Fish can swim. See them glide,
Swinging tails from side to side.
With a curve to the left and a curve to the right,
Moving quickly out of sight.

Fish can breathe. Fish can breathe.
They get oxygen that they need.
Into open mouths the chilly water spills,
Flowing out through pairs of gills.

Fish can rest. Fish can rest,
Moving slowly all the while.
With eyes open wide, fins flowing left and right,
Swimming slowly out of sight.

Life Science

Frog Life Cycle

These life cycle wheels help students explore how frogs develop and grow.

Materials for each student:
construction paper copy of the wheel patterns on pages 35 and 36
brad fastener

Steps:

1. Have each child cut out the bottom wheel pattern.
2. Read the text in each section and then give students the appropriate directions to follow.
   Section 1: Draw frog eggs near the plants.
   Section 2: Draw a tail on the tadpole.
   Section 3: Draw four legs on the tadpole.
   Section 4: Draw a lily pad under the frog.
3. Direct students to cut out the top wheel pattern. Then have each child draw a frog in the pond scene.
4. Have each child color the wheels, if desired.
5. Help each child use a brad to connect the top wheel and the bottom wheel.

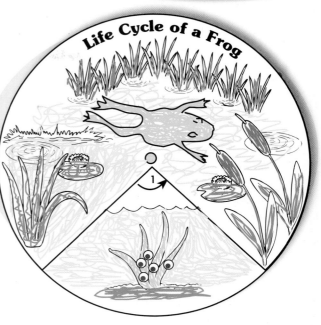

Life Cycle of a Frog

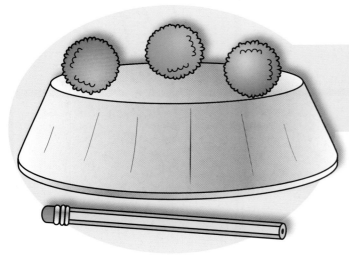

Feel the Vibrations

Materials:
picture of a real frog (profile view works best)
aluminum pie tin
small pom-poms
unsharpened pencil

To begin, share that some amphibians and reptiles hear by feeling vibrations that bounce off their eardrums. Display the picture and point out the eardrums. Then place the pie tin on the table upside down to represent the frog's ear. Invite one child to use the pencil to tap the tin as another child places one finger on the tin to feel the vibrations. Repeat with different students. To help youngsters see the effect of the vibrations, sprinkle a handful of small pom-poms on the tin and then have a child tap it again. Guide students to conclude that what they see and feel are similar to the sound vibrations that bounce off a frog's eardrums.

Did You Know?
A frog has an eardrum behind each eye. A frog's eardrum can also be called a tympanum.

Life Science

Animal Cards

Use with "Legs, Legs, Legs!" on page 12.

TEC61363

TEC61363

TEC61363

TEC61363

TEC61363

TEC61363

TEC61363

TEC61363

TEC61363

TEC61363

TEC61363

TEC61363

TEC61363

TEC61363

TEC61363

HOW MANY LEGS?

_____

name

20-Minute Science • ©The Mailbox® Books • TEC61363

Some animals have 2 legs.

1

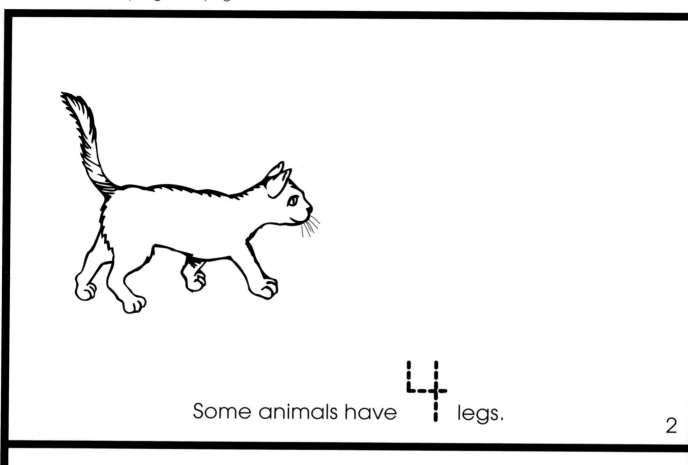

Some animals have 4 legs.

2

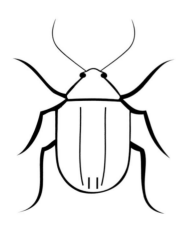

Some animals have 6 legs.

3

Some animals have 8 legs.

4

Some animals have 0 legs.

5

Perfect Pairs

 Cut.  Glue to match the baby with its parent.

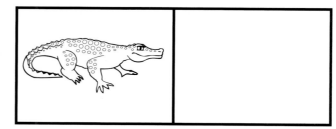

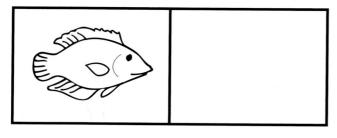

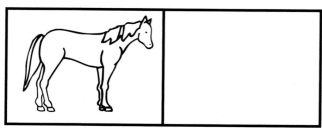

20-Minute Science • ©The Mailbox® Books • TEC61363

Note to the teacher: Use with "Growing and Changing" on page 14.

Name _____

Under Cover

 Cut. Sort. Glue.

fur 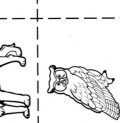	feathers	scales 

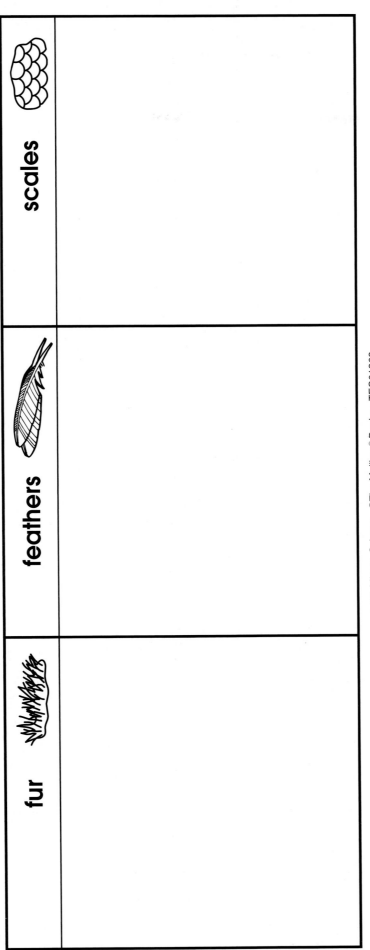

20-Minute Science • ©The Mailbox® Books • TEC61363

Note to the teacher: Use with "Animal Coverings" on page 14.

My Animal Report

 Circle.

Write.

Draw your animal under the flap.

I am   a mammal   a reptile   a fish   a bird   an insect

I am this color: _____.

I live here: _____.

I eat this: _____.

I make this sound: _____.

Can you guess what animal I am?

Tape.

I am a _____.

20-Minute Science • ©The Mailbox® Books • TEC61363

Note to the teacher: Use with "Riddle Reports" on page 14.

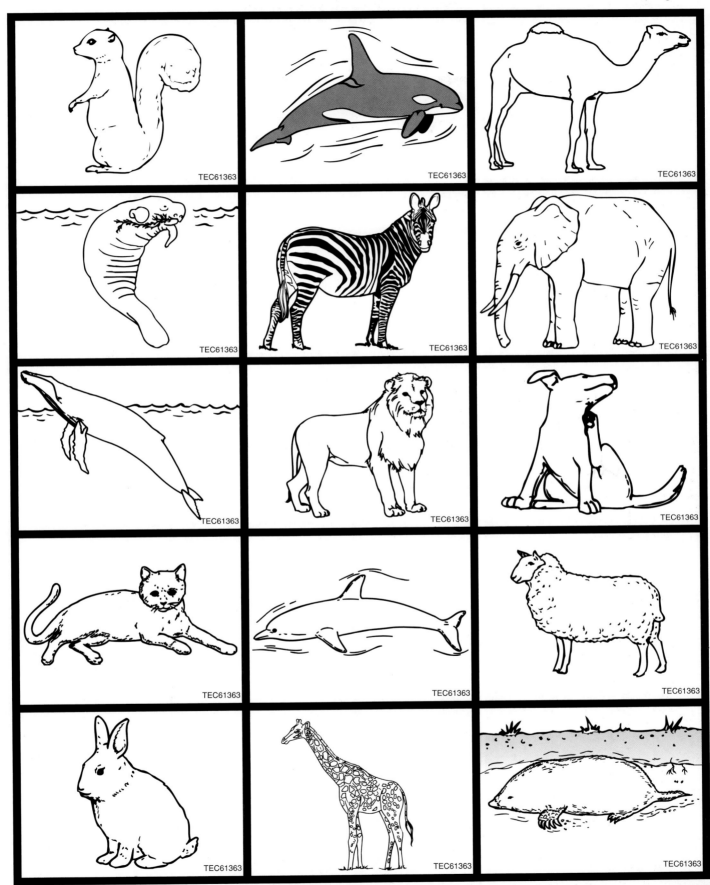

TEC61363

Baby to Adult Cards
Use with "From Baby to Adult" on page 16.

TEC61363

TEC61363

TEC61363

TEC61363

TEC61363

TEC61363

TEC61363

TEC61363

Name _____

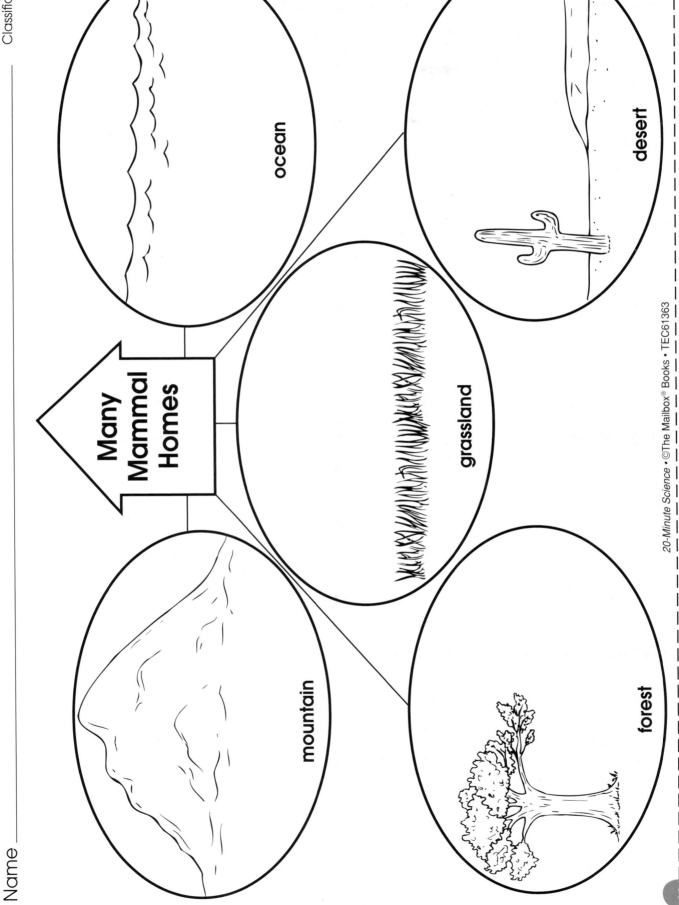

ocean

desert

Many Mammal Homes

grassland

mountain

forest

20-Minute Science • ©The Mailbox® Books • TEC61363

Note to the teacher: Use with "Home, Sweet Home" on page 16.

29

Card Sets

Use with "Bird Basics" on page 17.

20-Minute Science • ©The Mailbox® Books • TEC61363

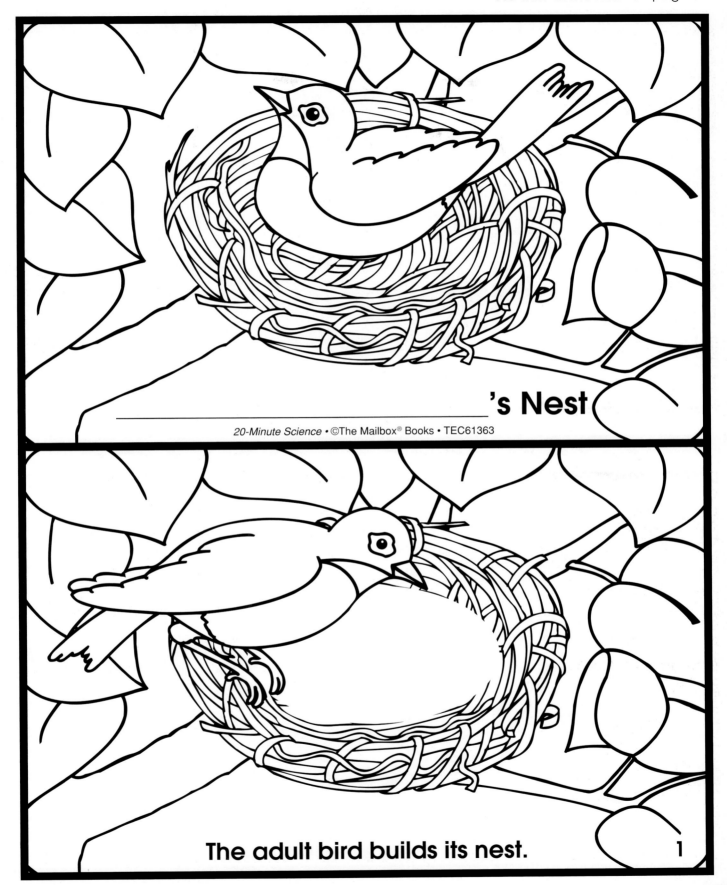

_____'s Nest

20-Minute Science • ©The Mailbox® Books • TEC61363

The adult bird builds its nest.

1

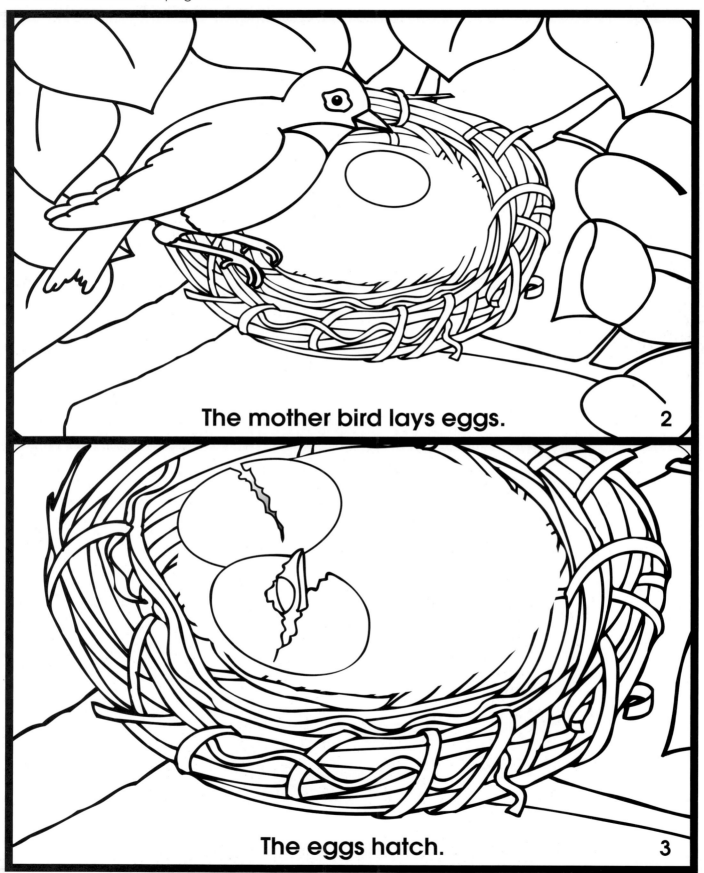

The mother bird lays eggs.

2

The eggs hatch.

3

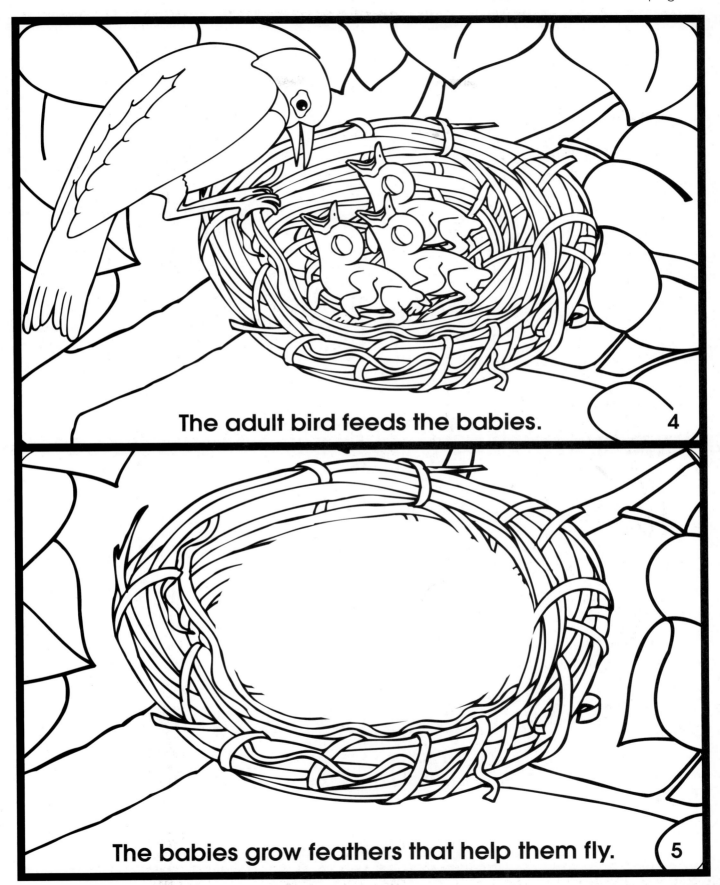

The adult bird feeds the babies.

4

The babies grow feathers that help them fly.

5

Fish Pattern and Word Cards

Use with "Fish Puppet" on page 18.

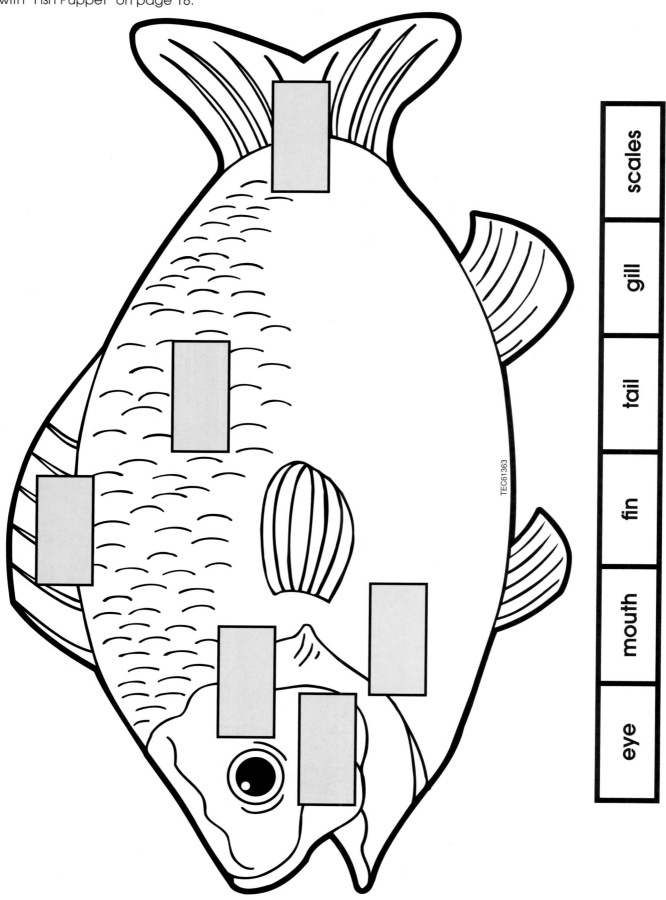

TEC61363

scales

gill

tail

fin

mouth

eye

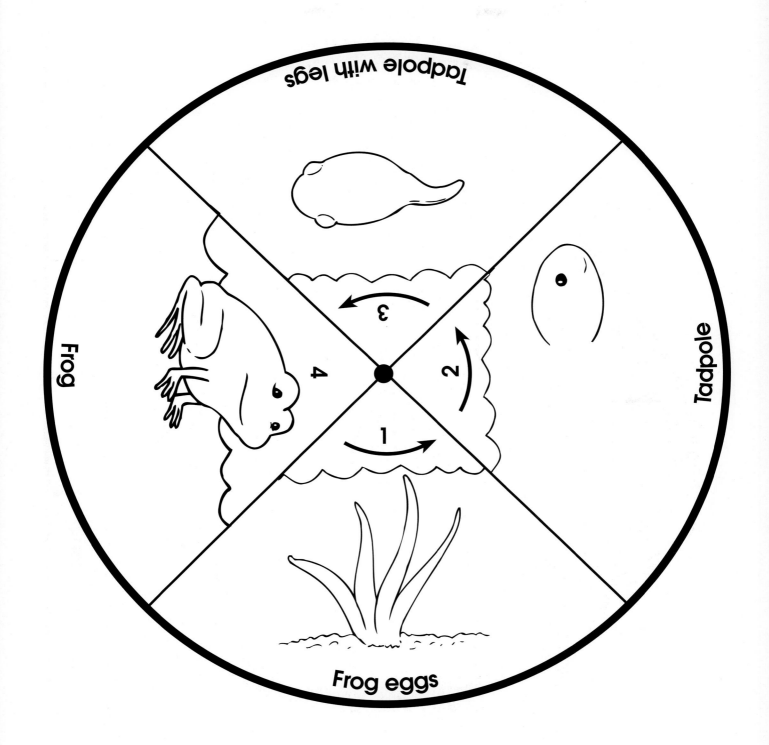

Tadpole with legs

Frog

Tadpole

Frog eggs

Top Wheel Pattern
Use with "Frog Life Cycle" on page 19.

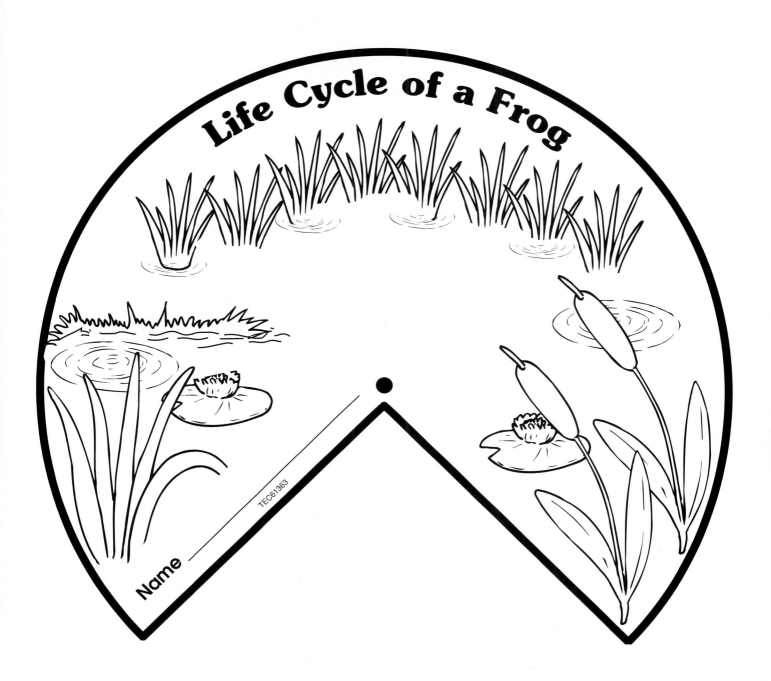

Life Cycle of a Frog

Name _____

TEC61363

Insects & Spiders

Part by Part

Materials for each student:
construction paper copy of the dragonfly
    pattern on page 44
jumbo craft stick
tape

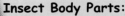

To make a puppet, have each child color and cut out the dragonfly pattern and tape the craft stick to the back of the cutout. Then describe different insect body parts. Ask each child to point to the insect part on his puppet. Invite a volunteer to name the body part.

Insect Body Parts:
- These are found near the eyes. An insect uses them to smell, feel, taste, or hear. *(antennae)*
- All insects have six of these. *(legs)*
- Insects sometimes have sticky pads on these to help them walk upside down. *(feet)*
- An insect uses these to fly and search for food or to escape from an enemy. *(wings)*
- An insect uses these to see. *(eyes)*

Bug Body Game

Materials for every two students:
2 copies of the bug pattern and card on page 44
die

Have each child cut out her bug pattern and card. Pair students. To play the game, each child lays her card faceup in front of her. In turn, each child rolls the die and colors the corresponding insect part on her bug. If a part is already colored, she loses a turn. Encourage partners to play until both insects are colored.

Insect or Spider?

Materials:
2 paper lunch bags, labeled as shown
construction paper copy of the insect and spider cards on
    page 45, cut apart

Place the bags in front of a small group and stack the cards facedown. Invite a volunteer to choose a card and show it to the group. Encourage the students to help the child decide whether the creature is an insect or a spider. Then have her place the card in the appropriate bag.

Life Science

Eating Aphids

Materials for each student:
white construction paper copy of page 46
brad fastener

Steps:

1. Tell students that aphids eat healthy plants. Then explain that ladybugs help plants because they eat aphids.
2. Have each child color and cut out the patterns.
3. Show students how to use the brad to connect the ladybug to the center of the leaf.
4. Invite each child to use his project to show a ladybug eating aphids.

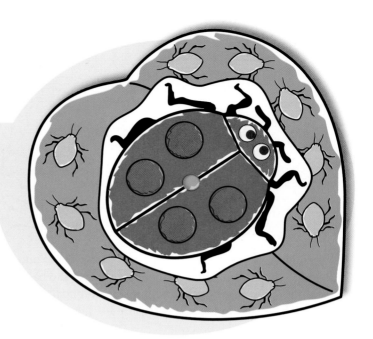

Insects in Our World

Sing this song to review the importance of insects. Invite students to brainstorm other ways insects are important as you list their ideas on the board.

(sung to the tune of "The Itsy-Bitsy Spider")

Itsy-bitsy helpers, you help us every day.
What would we do if you ever went away?
Bees give us honey, and ants work very hard.
Ladybugs eat aphids and leave a pretty yard.

Itsy-bitsy helpers, you help us every day.
What would we do if you ever went away?
Butterflies eat nectar and taste with their feet.
Grasshoppers eat leaves, and their jumping can't be beat!

Itsy-bitsy helpers, you help us every day.
What would we do if you ever went away?
Crickets give us music that makes us want to sing.
Oh, itsy-bitsy helpers, you do so many things!

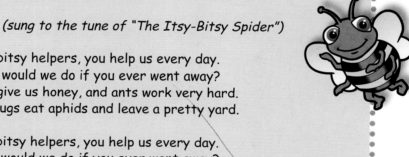 Life Science

sugar

salt

bread crumbs

cracker crumbs

Hungry Ants

Materials:
student copies of page 47
four jar lids
ant food (salt, sugar, bread crumbs, cracker crumbs)

Day 1: Place a bit of each food in a different labeled jar lid. Place the lids outdoors near an anthill or in an area that is likely to attract ants. Have students write and draw to predict which food they think the ants will like best.

Day 2: Several days after setting out the lids, have students revisit them to see which food the ants ate most. Then have youngsters record their findings on their observation sheets. Lead students in discussing if their predictions were correct.

Life in an Anthill

Materials for each student:
construction paper copy of pages 48 and 49
brad fastener

Steps:
1. Discuss with students the life cycle of an ant.
2. Have students color and cut out the wheel and cards and then glue the cards to the wheel in order.
3. Direct students to color the anthill on page 49. Help each child cut where indicated to make a window; then have him place the wheel behind the anthill so the dots are aligned.
4. Show students how to use the brad to connect the wheel behind the anthill.
5. Invite each child to gently turn the wheel as he explains the ant life cycle to a partner.

Name _____

Listen and do.

Life in an Anthill

Ant life cycle

adult

Life Science

Finding Food

Materials:
artificial or paper flowers
yellow pom-poms
empty container

Help youngsters learn how bees work together to feed the colony. In advance, place artificial flowers around the room. Put a handful of yellow pom-poms (pollen and nectar) near each flower. Set the container (beehive) in an open area. Invite students to hunt for pollen and nectar. When a child finds a flower, he takes one pom-pom and puts it in the hive. Then he visits a different flower. Continue until all the pollen and nectar is in the hive.

Did You Know?
Each worker bee gathers pollen and nectar from as many as 10,000 flowers a day.

Busy Bees

Teach students this fingerplay to remind them why bees make honey. Then discuss with youngsters other reasons bees are important.

One little honeybee,	*Hold up one finger.*
Buzzing all around,	*Make circular motion with finger.*
Spies a little flower	*Hold hand to forehead and look around.*
Growing from the ground.	*Push hand through opposite fist to represent growing flower.*
Sipping lots of nectar	
With its long, long tongue,	*Wiggle index finger.*
It brings nectar to its hive	*Make flying motion with index finger.*
To feed the hungry young.	*Wiggle fingers on opposite hand to represent baby bees.*
This tasty treat called honey	*Rub tummy.*
Is made by honeybees.	
And if we treat them kindly,	*Put hand on heart.*
They'll share with you and me.	*Point to another child and self.*

Life Science

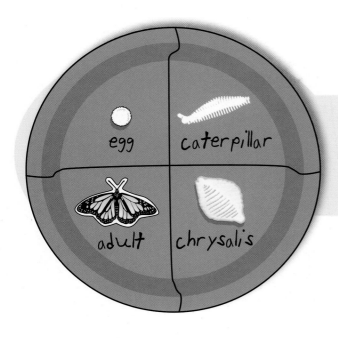

Life Cycle Model

Materials for each student:
butterfly sticker (or small cutout)
seashell pasta piece
green paper plate
small white pom-pom
section of white chenille bump stem
permanent marker

Steps for students:
1. Use the marker to divide the plate into four equal sections.
2. Label the quadrants as shown.
3. Glue each item to the appropriate quadrant.

A Beautiful Butterfly

Use this booklet activity to review the life cycle of a butterfly.

Materials for each student:
assembled copy of the booklet on pages 50–53
2 green construction paper leaf cutouts
white hole-punch dot
brown ink pad
hole puncher

Steps:
1. Have each child write his name on the booklet cover.
2. Read the text on a booklet page and then give students the appropriate direction to follow.
   Page 1: Color the leaf green. Glue the white dot to the leaf.
   Page 2: Draw and color a caterpillar with green and black stripes.
   Page 3: Punch three holes in one leaf and glue it to the page.
   Page 4: Punch ten holes in the remaining leaf and glue it to the page.
   Page 5: Color the branch brown. Make a brown fingerprint (chrysalis) below the branch.
   Page 6: Make a brown fingerprint (chrysalis) below the branch. Write "Zzzz." to show the caterpillar is resting.
   Page 7: Color the butterfly.

Life Science

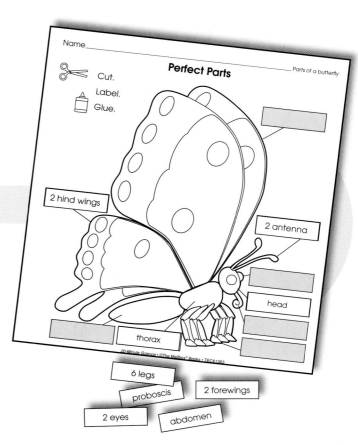

Name_____

Perfect Parts   Parts of a butterfly

✂ Cut.
💧 Label.
🧴 Glue.

2 hind wings

2 antenna

head

thorax

20-Minute Science • ©The Mailbox® Books • TEC61363

6 legs

proboscis   2 forewings

2 eyes   abdomen

Butterfly Parts

Materials:
class supply of page 54

As you describe and name each butterfly part, have students point to the corresponding part on the page. Then have each child cut out the cards on her copy of page 54. Guide students to glue each card in the correct box.

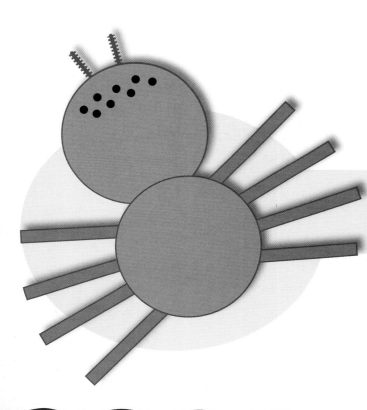

Amazing Spider Body

Materials for each student:
2 circle cutouts
2 small pieces of chenille stem (fangs)
8 construction paper strips (legs)
8 black hole-punch dots (eyes)

Steps for students:
1. Slightly overlap the two circles. Glue them together to make the spider body.
2. Glue the legs to the body.
3. Glue the fangs to the body; then set the project aside to dry.
4. When the glue is dry, turn the spider over and glue on the eyes.

Did You Know?
Spiders can have two, four, six, or eight eyes.

Life Science

Spider Life Cycle

Materials for each student:
copy of pages 55 and 56
brad fastener

Steps:

1. Have children color a copy of page 55 and color and cut out the patterns on a copy of page 56.
2. Show students how to poke the brad through the web cutout and then through the web on page 55; then show them how to fasten the brad.
3. Direct youngsters to glue the animal pictures in the appropriate spaces.
4. Invite students to turn the wheel to review the life cycle of a spider.
5. Discuss with students a spider's enemies and potential prey shown around the web.

Sticky Spiderwebs

Help students understand why spiders don't get stuck in their webs like other insects do.

Materials:
class supply of page 57
transparent double-sided tape

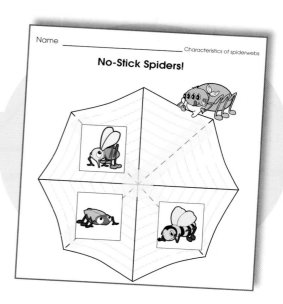

Steps:

1. Have students color and cut out a copy of page 57.
2. Have each child place two strips of the double-sided tape on the dotted web lines and place the insect cutouts on the tape. Explain that insects get stuck in the sticky strands of spiders' webs.
3. Invite students to point to where they think a spider could walk without getting stuck.
4. Explain to students that spiders can walk anywhere on their webs. They do not get stuck in the sticky strands of their webs because they have special oil in their feet.

Did You Know?
Spiderwebs have both dry and sticky strands of silk. Insects get caught and tangled in the sticky strands. Spiders don't stick to their webs because they walk on the dry strands and make a special oil for their feet so they don't stick to the sticky strands.

Life Science

Dragonfly Pattern
Use with "Part by Part" on page 37.

Bug Pattern and Cards
Use with "Bug Body Game" on page 37.

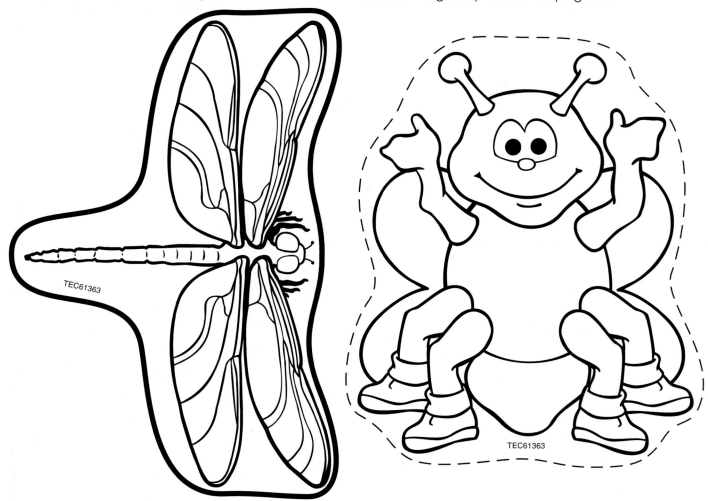

TEC61363

eyes

antennae

legs

body

wings

head

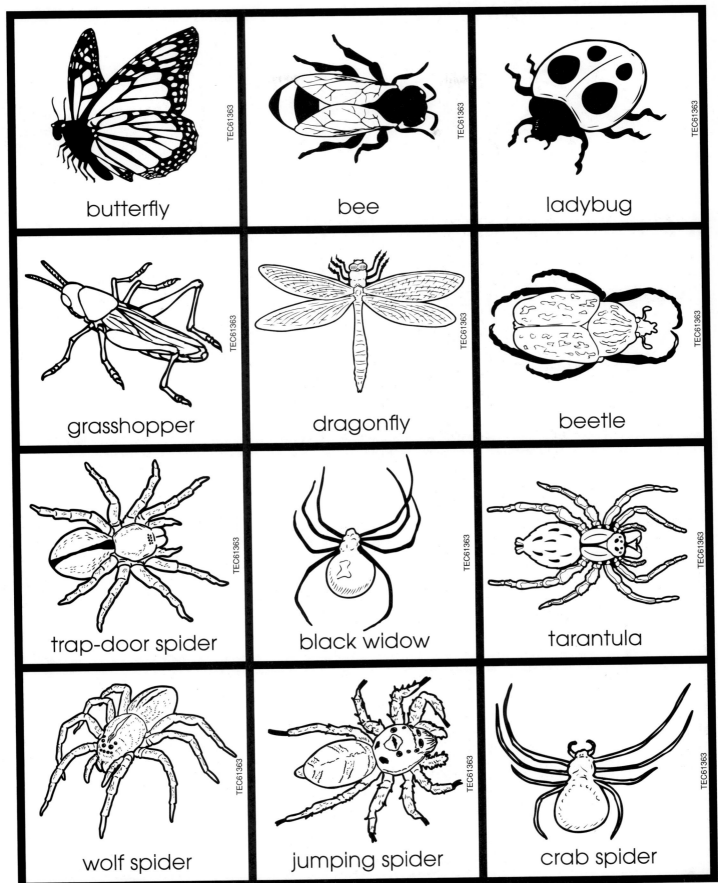

butterfly

bee

ladybug

grasshopper

dragonfly

beetle

trap-door spider

black widow

tarantula

wolf spider

jumping spider

crab spider

Ladybug and Leaf Patterns
Use with "Eating Aphids" on page 38.

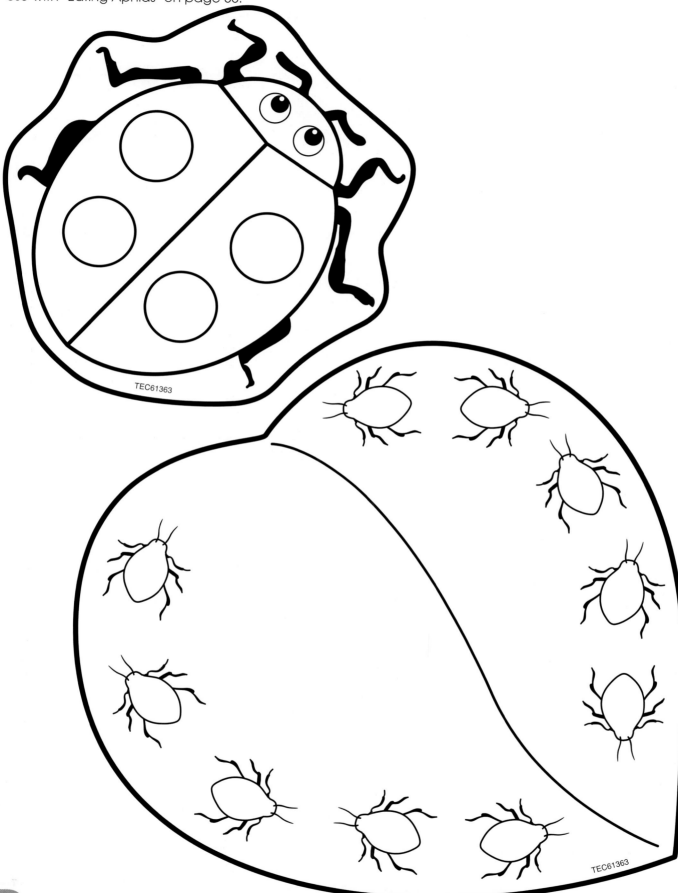

TEC61363

TEC61363

What to Eat?

I predict the ants will...

The ants actually...

20-Minute Science • ©The Mailbox® Books • TEC61363

Note to the teacher: Use with "Hungry Ants" on page 39.

Life Cycle Wheel and Cards

Use with "Life in an Anthill" on page 39.

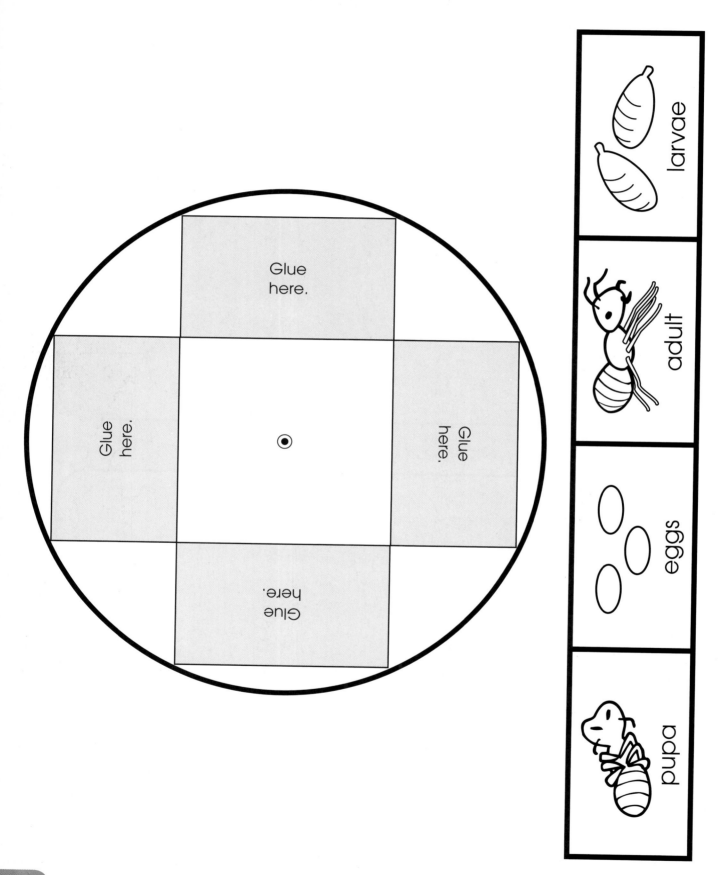

larvae

adult

eggs

pupa

Glue here.

Glue here.

Glue here.

Glue here.

Life in an Anthill

Listen and do.

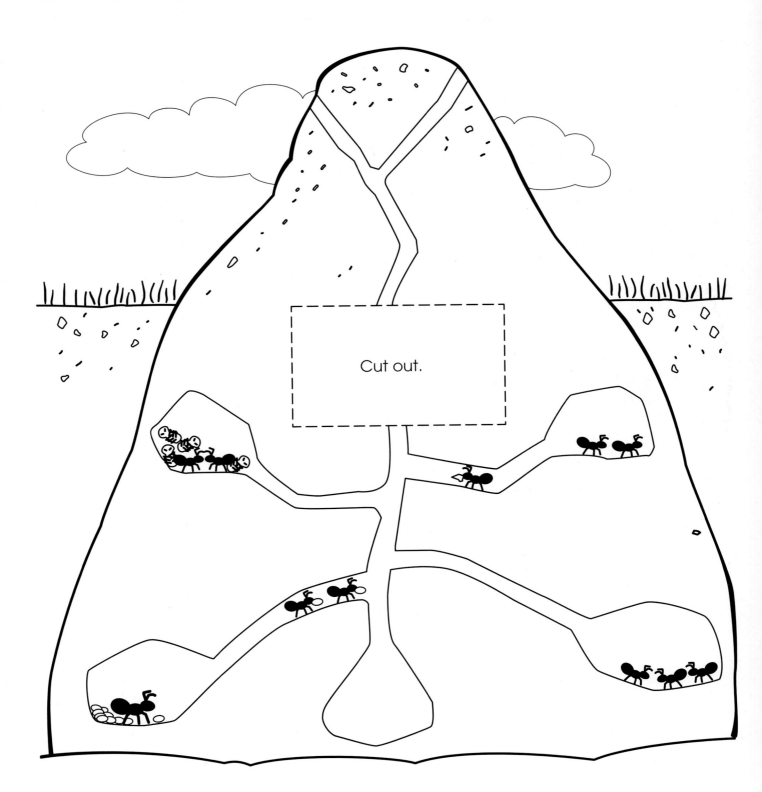

Cut out.

Note to the teacher: Use with "Life in an Anthill" on page 39.

A Beautiful Butterfly

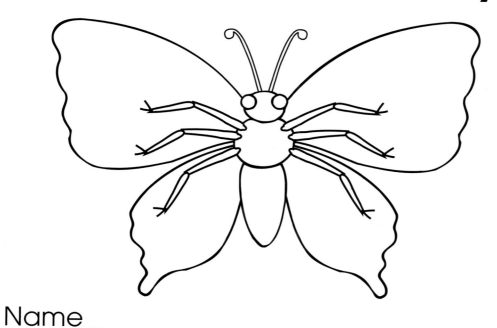

Name _____

20-Minute Science • ©The Mailbox® Books • TEC61363

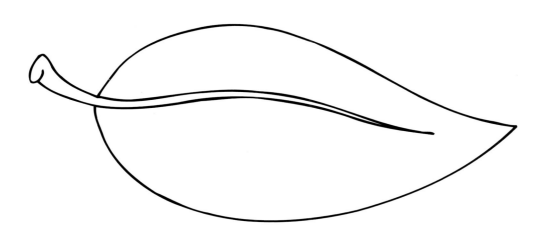

First, a tiny egg can be seen.

1

Next, there's a caterpillar, striped and green. 2

It eats and eats. Munch, munch, munch! 3

It eats some more.
Crunch, crunch, crunch!

4

Soon it's time to take a rest.
A chrysalis will work the best.

5

It'll sleep and sleep deep inside
Until it can no longer hide.

6

Then out pops a beautiful butterfly,
Just waiting for its wings to dry.

7

Perfect Parts

Cut.

Label.

Glue.

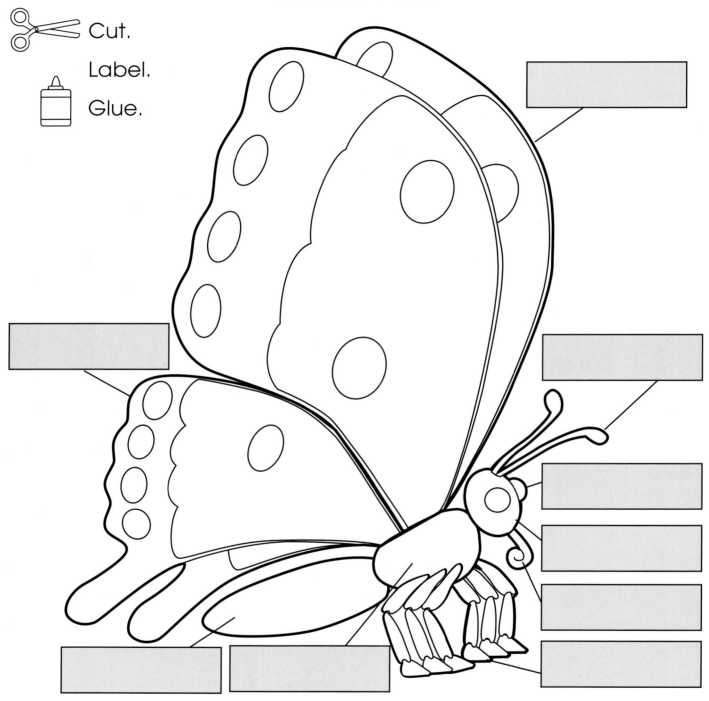

20-Minute Science • ©The Mailbox® Books • TEC61363

head	thorax	abdomen
2 forewings	2 hind wings	6 legs
proboscis	2 antennae	2 eyes

Note to the teacher: Use with "Butterfly Parts" on page 42.

The Life Cycle of a Spider

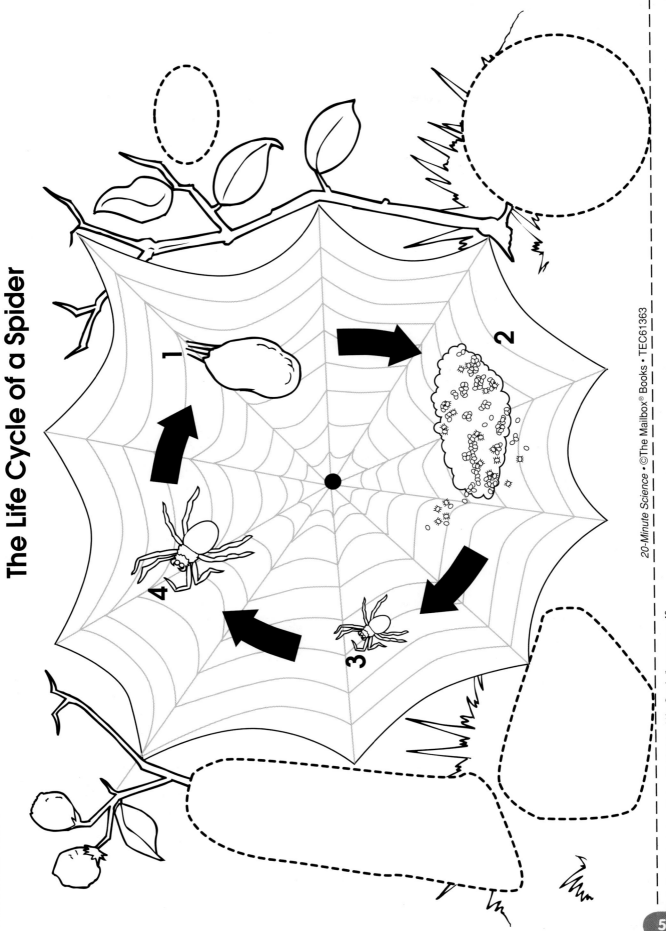

Note to the teacher: Use with "Spider Life Cycle" on page 43.

Web and Animal Patterns

Use with "Spider Life Cycle" on page 43.

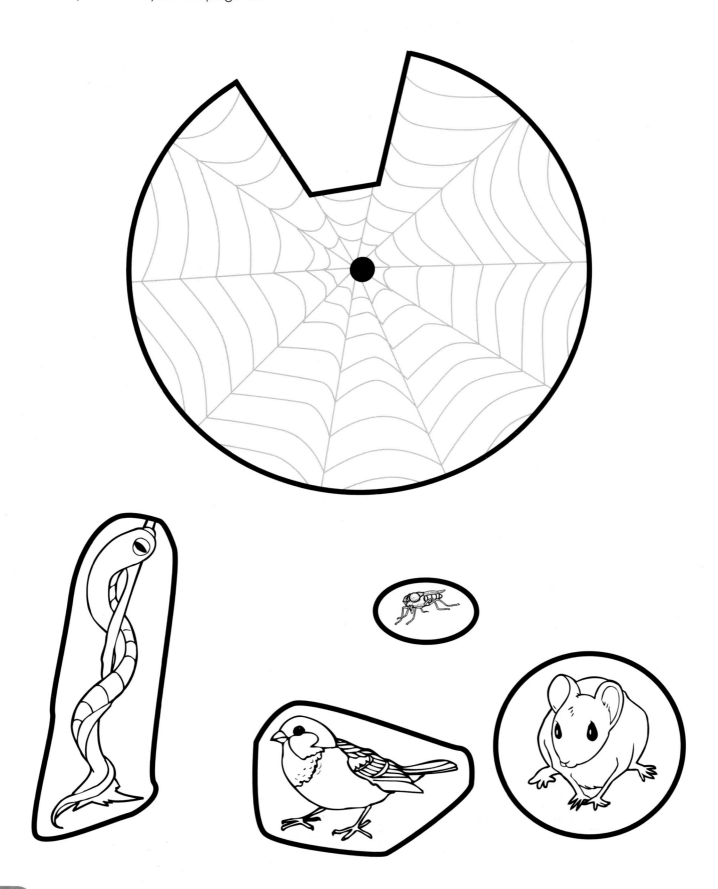

No-Stick Spiders!

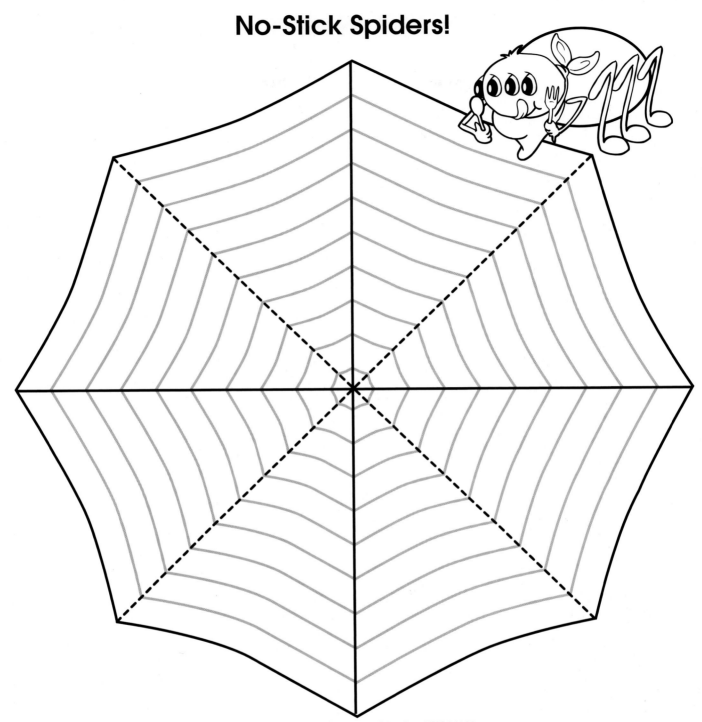

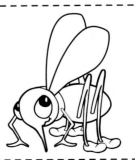

20-Minute Science • ©The Mailbox® Books • TEC61363

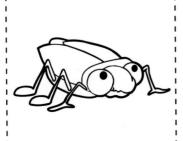

Note to the teacher: Use with "Sticky Spiders" on page 43.

Plants & Seeds

Plant Parts

Materials for each student:
assembled copy of the booklet project on pages 62–64

Steps:
1. Have each child write her name on the booklet cover. Then have her draw a vine and some leaves.
2. Read the text on a booklet page and then give students the appropriate direction to follow.
    - Page 1: Draw lines coming from the seed (roots).
    - Page 2: Draw a green stem coming from the seed.
    - Page 3: Draw leaves on the stem.
    - Page 4: Draw a flower on the stem. Draw seeds blowing in the wind.
    - Page 5: In each blank, write or dictate the name of the plant part.
3. Have students use their booklets to review the parts of a plant.

Grow, Plant, Grow!

Materials for each student:
soil
plant seeds
clear plastic cup
cards labeled as shown

Steps:
1. Discuss with students the needs of plants *(sun, water, air, space to grow)*.
2. Help each student put soil in a cup.
3. Direct each child to plant a seed close to the side of her cup (so the roots will be visible later).
4. Help each child water her seed and then place her cup in a sunny window.
5. Display the cards in the appropriate locations as you review the needs of a plant.
6. Encourage students to water their plants and check for growth daily.

Life Science

Inside a Seed

Materials:
class supply of dried lima beans soaked in red-tinted water
overnight *(The red food coloring makes it easier to
distinguish the seed parts.)*
magnifying glasses

Tell youngsters that seeds have three parts: the embryo,
the seed coat, and the food. Give each child a presoaked
bean on a paper towel and distribute the magnifying
glasses. Have each child carefully remove the seed coat
from his bean. Guide him to investigate the seed's interior
using a magnifying glass. Then help youngsters locate and
identify the seed parts as you sketch them on the board.

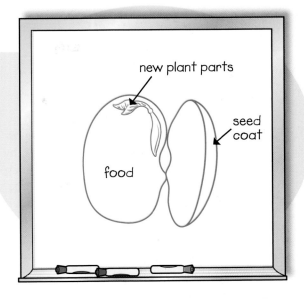

new plant parts

seed coat

food

Plant parts:
roots—hold the plant in the
soil and take in water and
minerals
stem—supports the flower
and leaves and carries
water
leaves—make food from
sunlight, water, and air
flower—has reproductive
parts that can help make
a new plant

Thirsty Plants

Materials for each student:
construction paper flower cutout (patterns on page 65)
with holes punched where indicated
cup of water
drinking straw

Discuss with students the parts of a plant
and their purposes as each child colors the
corresponding parts on her flower cutout. Then
direct each child to insert the straw in the holes in
her cutout. Give each child a cup of water. Invite
her to drink through her straw and pretend she is
a flower sipping minerals through her stem.

Life Science

Veggie Sort

Materials:
chart with the headings shown
pictures of vegetables

Discuss plant parts with students. Then display a picture of a vegetable and have students help classify it by the plant part it represents. Invite a volunteer to attach the picture to the appropriate section of the chart; then label the vegetable. Continue with each remaining vegetable picture.

Plant Parts				
roots	seeds	leaves	flower buds	fruit
carrot	peas	lettuce	broccoli	pepper
radish	corn	spinach	cauliflower	pumpkin
sweet potato		cabbage		

Growing Vegetable Soup

Plant the seeds.

Water the seeds and wait for the sun.

Watch the plants grow.

Pick the vegetables.

Wash and cut the vegetables.

Put the vegetables in a pot of water.

Cook the soup.

Growing Vegetable Soup

Materials:
class supply of page 66
class supply of blank 8-page booklets
8 sentence strips labeled as shown

Day 1: Lead students in a discussion about how to make vegetable soup. Then read aloud each sentence strip and have students help you sequence them to make a chart.

Day 2: Have each child color and cut out the cover label from a copy of page 66 and then cut out the sentence strips. Have each child sequence the strips, referring to the chart as needed. Direct him to glue the cover label to his booklet cover. Then have him glue each sentence strip on a separate page of his booklet. Ask him to illustrate each sentence and then share his booklet with a partner.

Life Science

Watermelon Life Cycle

After each student completes this picture wheel, read the text on each section aloud as a child spins the wheel to see the life cycle of a watermelon.

Materials for each student:
copy of page 67
9" red construction paper circle (with a wedge the size of one wheel section cut out)
brad fastener
green and black crayons

Steps for students:
1. Use the crayons to color a rind and seeds on the red circle so it looks like a watermelon.
2. Color and cut out the watermelon wheel.
3. Use the brad to attach the wheel behind the watermelon.

Plants Give Us...

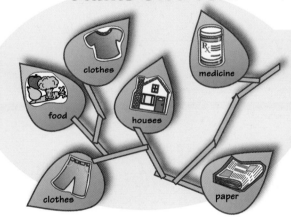

Useful Plants

Materials:
large leaf cutouts
magazines

Brainstorm with students different uses of plants such as those shown. Write each of their ideas on a separate leaf cutout. Then invite youngsters to cut out a magazine picture showing a plant use and glue it to the corresponding leaf. If desired, display the leaves along with green paper stems and a title similar to the one shown.

Plant Scavenger Hunt

Materials for every two students:
copy of page 68

Take youngsters outside to search for plants. Have the students in each pair mark their recording sheet each time they find an item. Later, have each pair count the marks for each item. Ask the students to draw a circle around the item found the most and a square around the item found the least. Discuss with youngsters the similarities and differences of those items found the most and those found the least.

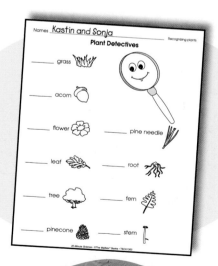

Life Science

Parts of a Plant

by _____

In the soil grow the roots.

1

The stem comes up as a tiny shoot.

2

The leaves make food so the plant can grow.

3

The flower has seeds that the wind blows.

4

Put them together, and what do you know?

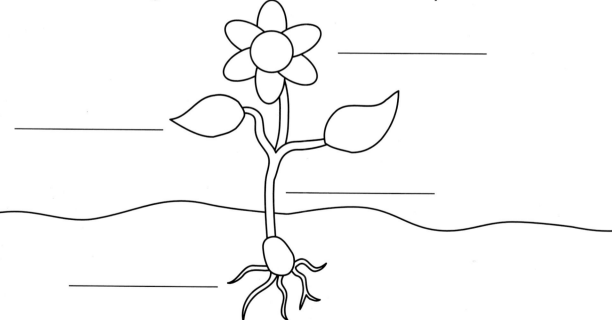

The parts of a plant will grow and grow!

5

20-Minute Science • ©The Mailbox® Books • TEC61363

Growing Vegetable Soup

by _____

20-Minute Science • ©The Mailbox® Books • TEC61363

Plant the seeds.

Pick the vegetables.

Water the seeds and wait for the sun.

Put the vegetables in a pot of water.

Wash and cut the vegetables.

Cook the soup.

Watch the plants grow.

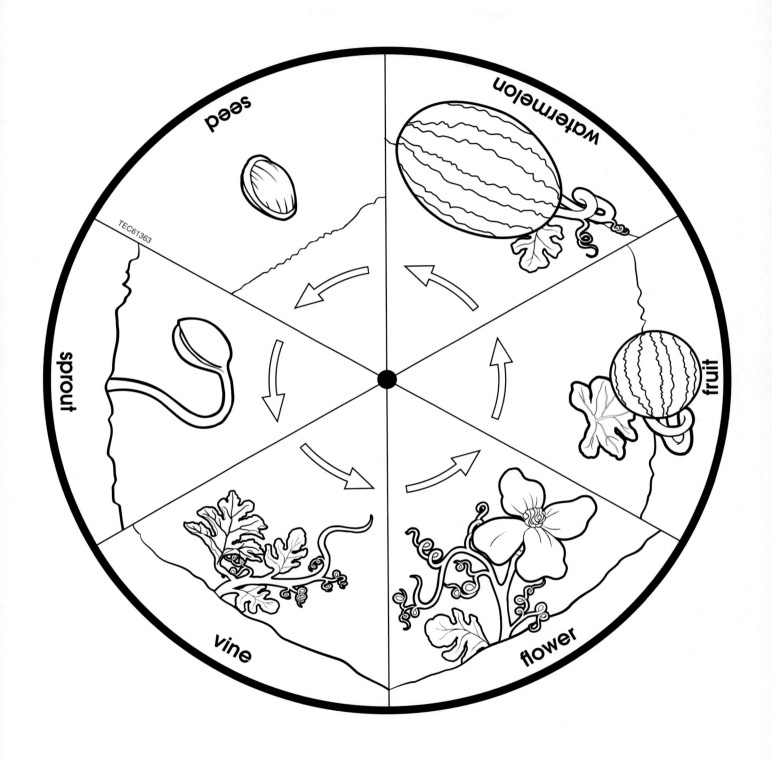

seed

watermelon

sprout

fruit

TEC61363

vine

flower

Plant Detectives

_____ grass

_____ acorn

_____ flower    _____ pine needle

_____ leaf    _____ root

_____ tree    _____ fern

_____ pinecone    _____ stem

Note to the teacher: Use with "Plant Scavenger Hunt" on page 61.

Leaves & Trees

Lovely Leaves

Materials for each small group:
variety of leaves

Invite each group to observe the color, shape, size, texture, and smell of the leaves. Then ask each group to determine if the leaves came from the same plant. Have students in each group, in turn, share their conclusion and observations that support it.

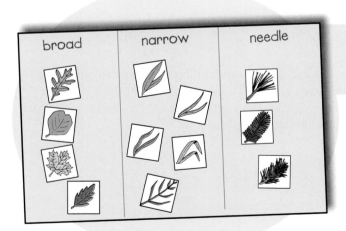

Leaf-Shape Sort

Materials:
copy of the picture cards on page 73, colored and cut apart
example of each type of leaf shape (broad, narrow, and needle)
sheet of bulletin board paper, labeled as shown

Explain to students that most leaves can be sorted into three different groups according to their shape: broad, narrow, or needle. Display each type of leaf and compare each shape with youngsters. Show students each picture card, in turn, and invite a volunteer to attach it to the appropriate column on the chart.

Life Science

Life of a Leaf

Your youngsters may be surprised to learn that leaves have a life cycle, just like people and animals do!

Materials for each student:
copy of page 74

Discuss with students how leaves change during each season. Then have each child color and cut out the cards on the bottom of page 74. Help students sequence the cards; then have each child glue her cards in place.

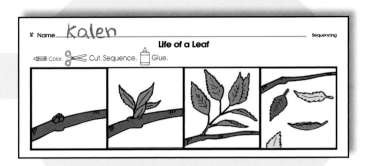

Mighty Oak Tree

Reinforce the concept of the life cycle of a tree with this fun action rhyme.

Materials for each student:
copy of page 75
6" x 18" construction paper strip

Day 1: Review the life cycle of a tree with students. Then lead them in performing the action rhyme shown.

Day 2: Lead students in reciting the action rhyme again. Then have each child color and cut apart the cards on a copy of page 75. Have him sequence the cards on a paper strip and glue them in place.

seed	seedling	sapling	tree

The mighty oak tree stands strong and tall. *Stand straight with arms extended.*
Storms may blow, but it does not fall. *Sway body back and forth.*
An acorn drops to the ground. *Roll into a ball.*
Soon a sapling will be found. *Slowly raise one hand.*
This new oak tree will grow, grow, grow! *Slowly straighten up, stretching out arms.*

Life Science

Healthy Tree Snacks

Materials for each student:
paper plate
several broccoli florets
pretzel stick
three chow mein noodles

Steps:

1. Review the main parts of a tree *(leaves, trunk and branches, and roots)* with students.
2. Have each child arrange the materials so they resemble a tree, as shown.
3. Invite each child to name each part of his tree as he enjoys his snack.

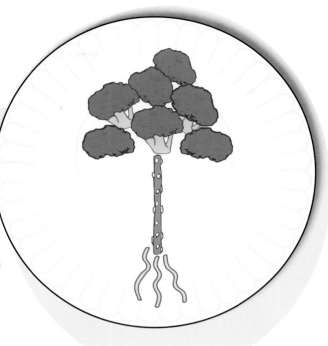

Treetop Homes

Materials for each student:
copy of page 76

Lead students in discussing why a tree makes a good home for some animals. Next, on a copy of page 76, have each child color and cut out the animal cards and then glue in place each animal that lives in a tree.

Did You Know?
Trees can provide animals with food, protection, and a place to sleep.

Life Science

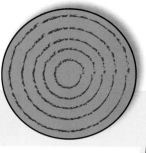

A Growing Tree

Materials for each student:
copy of page 77
6" light brown construction paper circle

Day 1: Explain to students that counting the rings on a tree shows the age of the tree. Then guide students as they each complete a copy of page 77.

Day 2: Remind students that a tree continues to grow throughout its life. Then give each child a construction paper circle to represent a tree stump. Have each child make the tree his own age by drawing a ring on the stump for each year of his life.

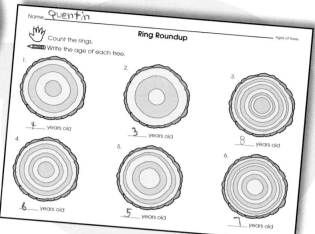

Matt

Tree Protection

Explain to students that the bark of a tree protects its inner layers, much like skin protects the inside of a human body. Then lead youngsters in completing the project below.

Materials for each student:
copy of page 78
12" x 18" sheet of construction paper
tan and brown construction paper scraps

Steps for students:
1. Color and cut out the bottom trunk. Glue it to the center of the construction paper (positioned vertically).
2. Color and cut out the remaining trunk. Cut it in half along the dotted line.
3. Place glue on the outer edges of each trunk half. Glue them to the other trunk as shown.
4. Tear the construction paper scraps into small pieces (bark). Glue the bark to each trunk half.
5. Draw a crown on your tree.
6. When the glue dries, open the tree trunk to reveal the layer below the bark.

Life Science

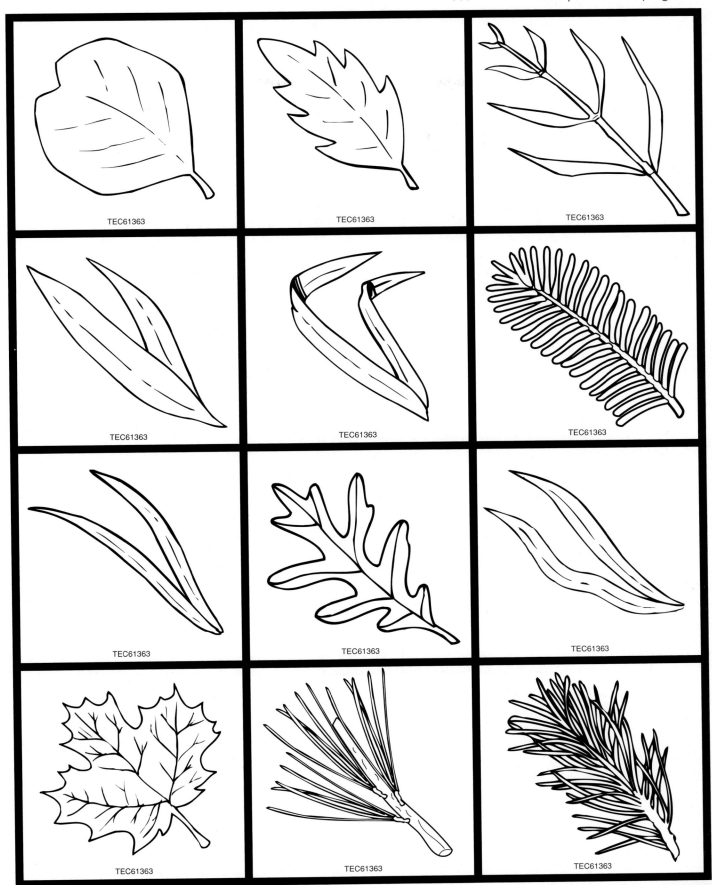

TEC61363

TEC61363

TEC61363

TEC61363

TEC61363

TEC61363

TEC61363

TEC61363

TEC61363

TEC61363

TEC61363

TEC61363

Name _____

Life of a Leaf

✂ Cut. Sequence. 🏺 Glue.

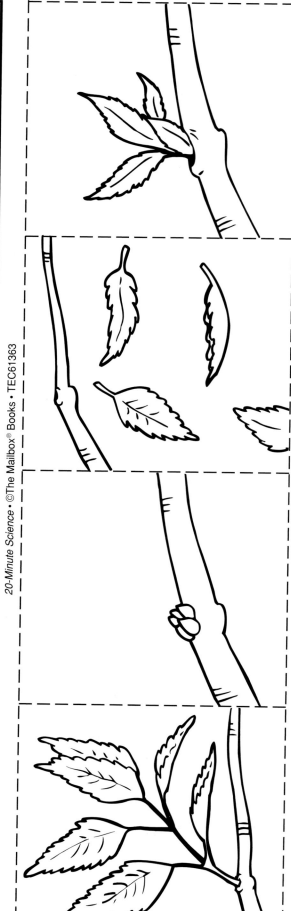

20-Minute Science • ©The Mailbox® Books • TEC61363

Note to the teacher: Use with "Life of a Leaf" on page 70.

tree

TEC61363

seedling

TEC61363

seed

TEC61363

sapling

TEC61363

Welcome Home!

✂ Cut. 🧴 Glue.

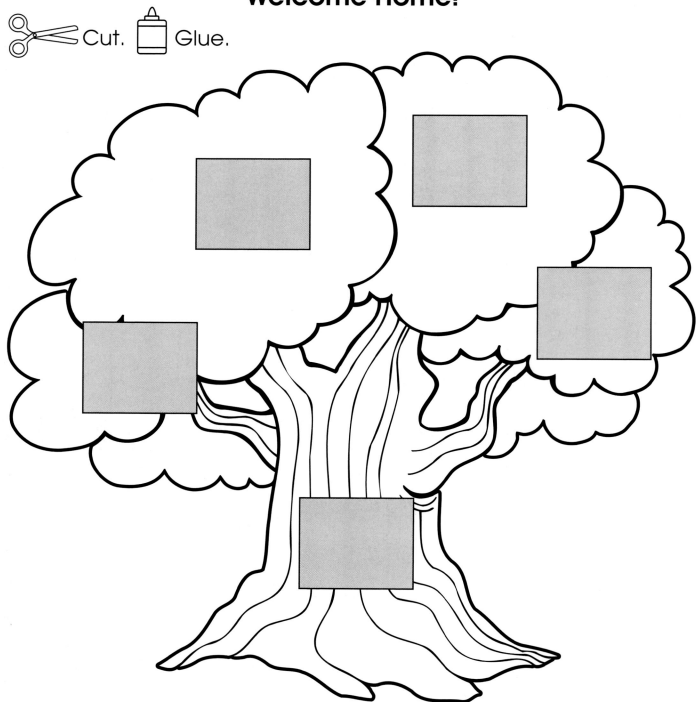

Bonus: Draw and color a different animal that makes its home in a tree.

20-Minute Science • ©The Mailbox® Books • TEC61363

 owl   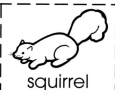 squirrel   bird   monkey   fish   raccoon

Note to the teacher: Use with "Treetop Homes" on page 71.

Name _____

Ring Roundup

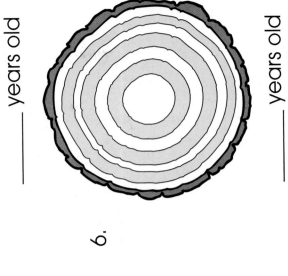

Count the rings.

Write the age of each tree.

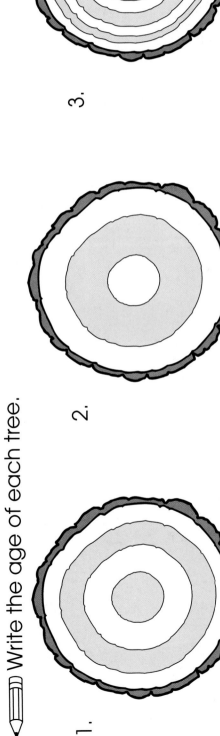

1.

2.

3.

_____ years old

4.

_____ years old

5.

_____ years old

6.

_____ years old

_____ years old

Note to the teacher: Use with "A Growing Tree" on page 72.

77

Trunk Patterns

Use with "Tree Protection" on page 72.

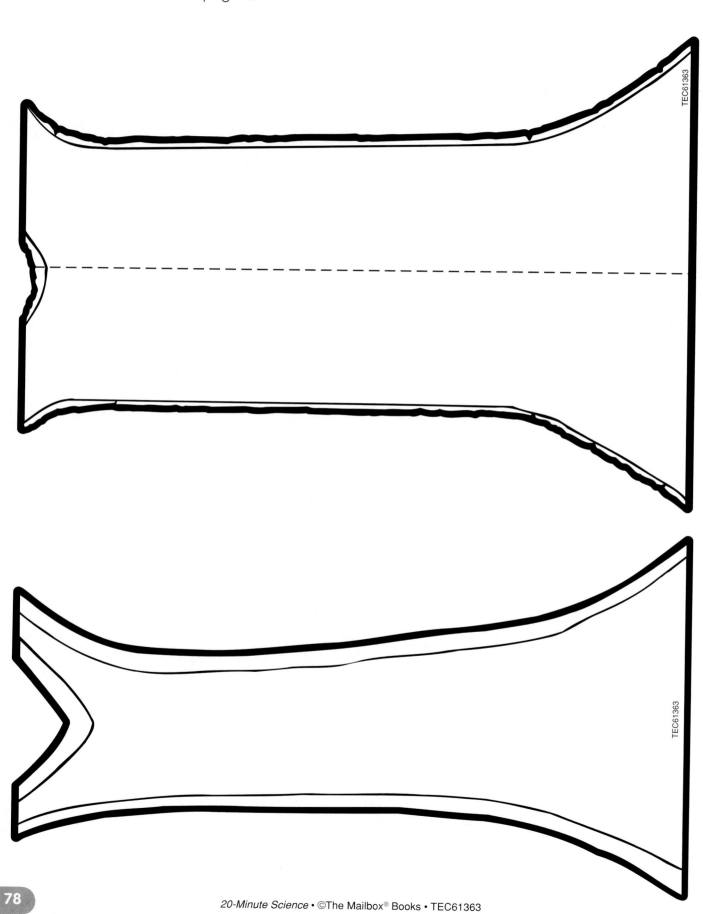

Colorful Sorting

Materials:
class supply of copies of page 83
variety of objects in three different colors
chart, similar to the one shown, labeled with appropriate colors

Day 1: Invite children to sort the items into color groups. Write the name of each item in the appropriate column of the chart. If desired, draw a quick sketch of each item.

Day 2: Discuss the results of the chart with youngsters. Then have each child complete a copy of page 83 as a follow-up activity.

purple	yellow	red
backpack	pencil	apple
grapes	smiley face	fire truck
paintbrush	paper	

Leaf Match-Ups

Materials:
several leaves of varying sizes and shapes

Use leaves to help youngsters practice matching by size and shape. To prepare, trace the outline of each leaf on a separate sheet of paper. Sit with students in a circle and scatter the leaf outlines inside the circle. Show youngsters a leaf and ask volunteers to make observations about its size and shape. Then have students find the corresponding outline. Ask a volunteer to lay the leaf atop the outline to check for accuracy. Continue with each remaining leaf.

Physical Science

Texture Match

Materials:
different texture words written on blank cards
class supply of small objects of different textures (sandpaper, cotton, feathers, buttons, paper clips, etc.)
large paper bag

Place the objects in the paper bag. Sit with students in a circle and spread the cards out in the center. Review the different textures with students. Then have each child, in turn, take an item from the bag. After she determines its texture, have her place the object below the corresponding card.

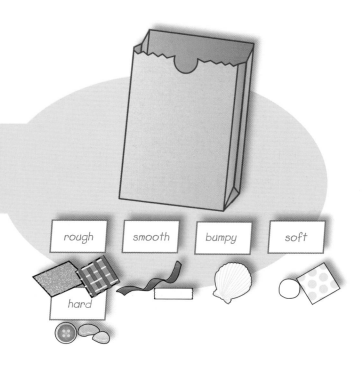

Touchable Quilt

Materials:
class supply of 9" construction paper squares
supply of objects with different textures

Students explore different textures as they make squares for a class quilt display. Have each student personalize his paper square and then glue a variety of objects of different textures to it. Display the completed squares as shown; then use a marker to add stitching details.

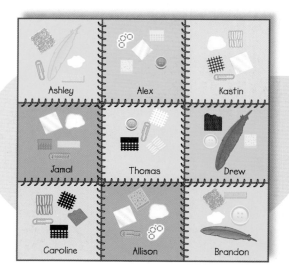

Classifying Objects

Materials for each student:
copy of page 84

Have each child locate objects in the classroom that she can classify using one or more of her senses. Then have her draw each object in the appropriate section on her copy of page 84. If desired, invite students to share their classifications with their classmates.

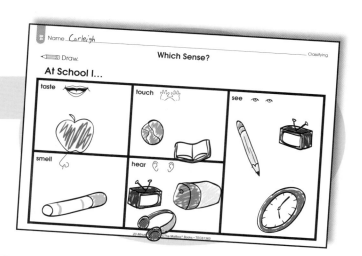

PhysicaL ScIeNce

What Is It?

Explain to students that scientists use physical properties to describe matter. List the most common properties on the board (*weight*, *color*, *hardness*, *shape*, *size*, *taste*, and *smell*). Then have each student secretly choose an item in the classroom. Invite a volunteer to name several physical properties of his object. Then encourage the other students to guess what the object is. After the object has been identified, encourage another youngster to share the properties of her object.

It is the door!

It is very hard.
It is brown.
It is very big.
It is a rectangle.
It is heavy.

They're all hard!

Property Practice

Materials for every two students:
paper lunch bag

Invite each pair of students to collect several items that collectively fit inside the bag and share a common physical property. Next, have each duo pair up with another twosome and trade bags. Each pair removes the objects from the bag and determines the items' common property. When both pairs have made correct identifications, the collections are returned to the bags. Then each twosome trades bags with another duo. Continue in this manner as time allows.

Physical Science

Solids and Liquids

Materials:
chart like the one shown, labeled with headings and questions
2 resealable plastic bags—one with a colorful block inside,
   one with tinted water inside

Show students the bags and ask them to identify
the type of matter represented in each one. Next, use
the bags to help students discover the answer to each
question on the chart. When all the answers are recorded,
lead students in discussing the results.

Matter	Solid	Liquid
Does it take up space?	Yes	Yes
Does it have weight?	Yes	Yes
Is it visible?	Yes	Yes
Can it change shape easily?	No	Yes

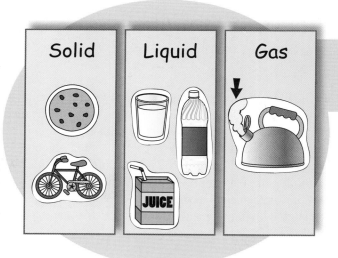

Which State of Matter?

Materials:
3 charts, each labeled as shown
magazines with pictures
tape

Ask each student to cut a picture from a magazine.
Then have each child, in turn, name her pictured item and
its state of matter and tape the picture to the appropriate
chart. (If no magazine pictures are found for the gas chart,
invite volunteers to draw pictures.)

Physical Science

Name _____

A Colorful Garden

 Color by the code.

 Count.

 Color the graph.

Color Code

 1 red   1 yellow

2 yellow   2 orange

3 orange   3 red

4 green   5 blue

Colors of Plants and Animals

	blue	red	orange	yellow	green
5					
4					
3					
2					
1					

Number colored

Colors

Note to the teacher: Use with "Colorful Sorting" on page 79.

84

Which Sense?

✏️ Draw.

At School I...

taste 👄	touch ✋	see 👁️
smell 👃	hear 👂	

Note to the teacher: Use with "Classifying Objects" on page 80.

Magnets

Is It Magnetic?

Materials:
class supply of page 87
magnet
objects listed on page 87 (one of each)

Show students an object and have each child predict whether it is magnetic. Then direct her to make a check mark in the appropriate column on her page. Next, ask a volunteer to test the object with the magnet. In the last column on her page, have each child draw a smiley face or a sad face to correspond with the accuracy of her prediction. Continue with each remaining object. Finally, lead youngsters in a discussion about the characteristics of magnetic and nonmagnetic objects.

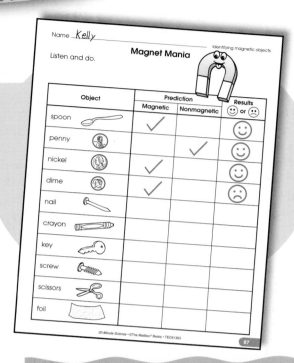

Name _Kelly_

Listen and do.

Magnet Mania

Identifying magnetic objects

Object	Prediction		Results
	Magnetic	Nonmagnetic	☺ or ☹
spoon	✓		☺
penny		✓	☺
nickel	✓		☺
dime	✓		☹
nail			
crayon			
key			
screw			
scissors			
foil			

20-Minute Science • ©The Mailbox® Books • TEC61363 87

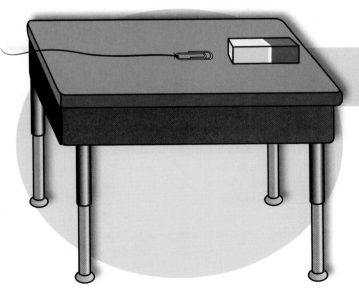

On the Move

Materials for every two students:
magnet
jumbo paper clip with string attached

Direct each student pair to rest its paper clip on a desktop. Then challenge each duo to move the paper clip across the desktop without touching the string or the paper clip. After a predetermined amount of time, gather students and have each duo share its results.

Physical Science

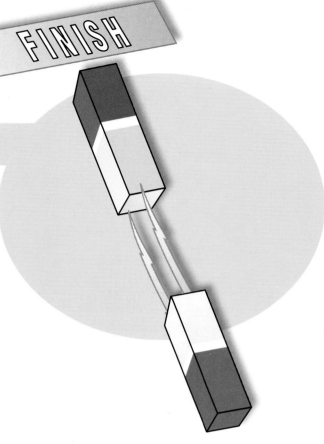

Magnet Races

Materials for every four students:
4 bar magnets

Tell students that like poles on magnets will repel each other, causing the magnets to move away from each other. Then have each group stand at a table with two students on each side. Have each student on one side of the table place a magnet on the edge of the table. Next, have him use the other magnet to race (repel) the first magnet across the table. Then invite the students on the other side to repeat the process to race the magnets back.

Will It Attract?

Materials:
class supply of page 88
strong magnet
jumbo paper clips
shallow container of paper shreds
shallow container of sand
plastic bottle of water

To prepare, nestle some paper clips in the paper shreds and some in the sand. Also drop some paper clips in the bottle of water and secure the cap. Remind students that magnets attract paper clips. Then ask students whether they think the magnet will attract the paper clips in the paper shreds. After each youngster shares his thoughts, run the magnet over the top of the paper shreds and show youngsters what happens. Have each child circle the appropriate picture on his copy of page 88. Repeat this process with the container of sand and the bottle of water. Finally, lead youngsters to conclude that the magnet will attract the paper clips through each of the materials.

Physical Science

Name _____

Magnet Mania

Listen and do.

Object	Prediction		Results
	Magnetic	Nonmagnetic	☺ or ☹
spoon			
penny			
nickel			
dime			
nail			
crayon			
key			
screw			
scissors			
foil			

20-Minute Science • ©The Mailbox® Books • TEC61363

Note to the teacher: Use with "Is It Magnetic?" on page 85.

Will It Attract?

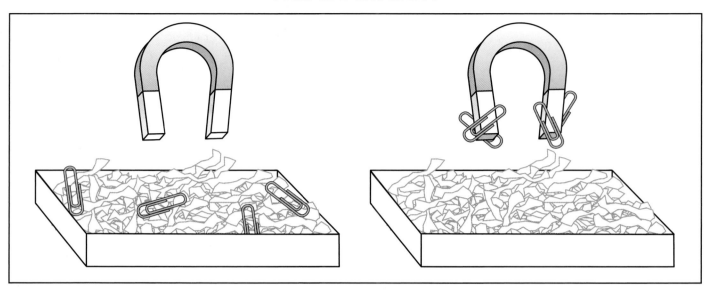

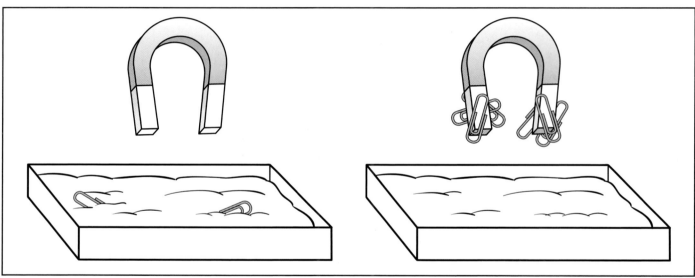

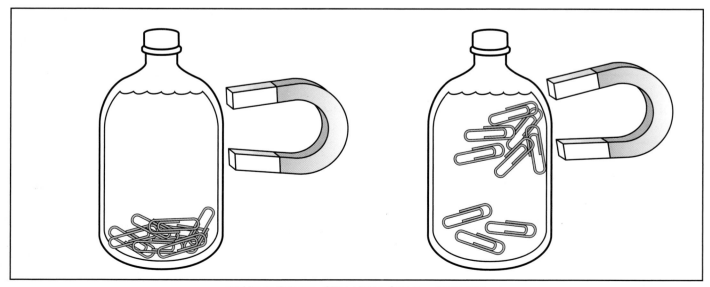

Note to the teacher: Use with "Will It Attract?" on page 86.

Digging Into Rocks

Materials:
2 rock-shaped cutouts
collection of rocks in a variety of shapes, sizes, colors, and
   textures

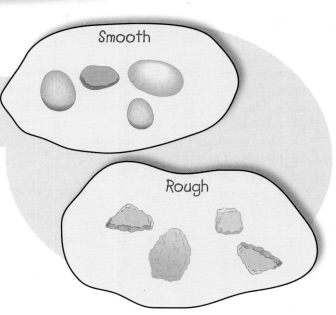

To begin, invite a small group of students to brainstorm
rock characteristics as you list their ideas on the board.
Help students choose a pair of characteristics and
write each one on a separate rock cutout. Allow time
for youngsters to explore the rock collection. Then ask
volunteers to sort each rock onto the appropriate cutout.
Repeat the process with different small groups. Have each
group choose different characteristics to sort the rocks by.

Rock Report

Materials:
assembled copy of the booklet on pages 93 and 94 for each student
small rock for each student
magnifying glasses
magnets
container of water

Set up three rock exploration centers. Place the magnifying
glasses at one center, the magnets at another center, and the
container of water at the third center. Give a rock to each
child. Then invite her to visit each center, in turn, and use the
directions shown to complete her booklet.

Directions
- **Cover:** Draw a picture of your rock in the box.
- **Page 1:** Use a magnifying glass to examine your rock. Draw your rock. Complete each sentence.
- **Page 2:** Use a magnet to test your rock. Write *did* or *did not* in the blank and complete the next sentence.
- **Page 3:** Draw a picture of your rock in the water. Write *sinks* or *floats* in the blank.

Earth & Space Science

Nature Detectives

Materials for each student:
copy of page 95

To begin, discuss with students the difference between man-made and natural items. Then take youngsters outside. (If an outdoor area is not available, have students complete the activity while looking out of a window.) Invite each child to find examples of natural and man-made items and draw a picture of each item in the appropriate section of his paper.

Our Earth

Lead youngsters in singing this toe-tapping tune. After singing, guide students to discuss other ways they can help the planet as you list their ideas on the board.

(sung to the tune of "This Land Is Your Land")

This earth is your earth.
This earth is my earth.
And we can all help
To preserve its worth.
We can recycle
And pick up litter.
Keep this earth clean for you and me.

When I see trees grow,
I smile, for I know
They make the air clean
And keep the world green.
Each and every day,
I cheer and I say,
"Keep this earth clean for you and me."

The Three Rs

Materials for each student:
assembled copy of the booklet on pages 96 and 97

To begin, discuss with students the difference between reducing, reusing, and recycling. Then have each child write her name on her booklet cover. For each booklet page, read the word and definition aloud. Then have each child draw a picture to show an example of each word.

Did You Know?
The average American produces about three pounds of trash every day.

Earth & Space Science

Objects in the Sky

Sun Study

To begin, tell students that they should never look directly at the sun. Explain that studying the sun's reflection is a safer way to get a look at the sun. Then divide the class into groups of three and guide them through the following activity.

Materials for every three students:
plastic mirror covered with a yellow piece of paper that has a hole poked in its middle
9" x 12" white construction paper

Steps:
1. Have one group member hold the paper-covered mirror and stand facing the sun.
2. Ask a second group member to hold the white paper and stand with his back to the sun, about three feet away from the first group member.
3. Have the child holding the mirror adjust it until the sun's image is reflected on the white paper.
4. Invite the third group member to study the reflection of the sun on the white paper.
5. Have youngsters change places and repeat the experiment until each child has had a turn looking at the sun's reflection.

Sun Collage

Remind students that all living things depend on the sun to survive. Then have each child make a collage showcasing some items that rely on the sun.

Materials for each student:
8" yellow construction paper circle
yellow construction paper
orange construction paper
magazines

Steps for students:
1. Look through magazines and cut out pictures of things that depend on the sun to survive, such as plants, animals, and people.
2. Glue the pictures to the yellow circle.
3. Cut thin triangles (rays) from each sheet of construction paper.
4. Glue the rays around the outer edge of the circle as shown.

Earth & Space Science

By the Light of the Moon

Materials:
flashlight
plastic mirror
ball

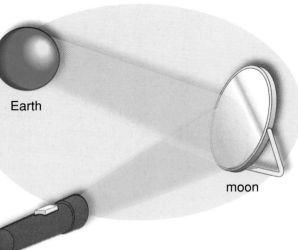

Earth

moon

sun

To begin, ask students if they think the moon produces its own light or if they think the light comes from something else. Then ask three volunteers to each hold one of the materials. Dim the lights and instruct the child holding the flashlight (sun) to shine it on the mirror (moon). Direct the student holding the ball (Earth) to position it so that it catches the light reflected off the mirror. From this demonstration, lead students to realize that the light actually comes from the sun and is reflected off the surface of the moon.

Sun	Moon
〰〰 〰〰 〰〰 〰〰	〰〰 〰〰〰 〰〰 〰〰 〰〰〰 〰〰 〰〰〰
	〰〰 〰〰〰

Sun and Moon

Materials:
assembled copy of the booklet project on page 98 for each
      student
chart paper, labeled as shown

For each booklet page, read the text aloud and have students complete the sentence with a word from the word bank. Then invite each child to share something he knows about the sun or the moon as you list it in the appropriate column of the chart.

Where Do the Stars Go?

Materials:
flashlight

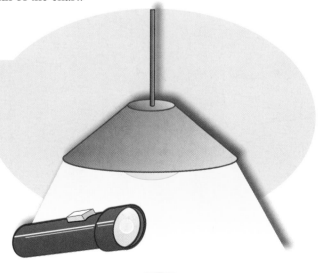

Dim the classroom lights; then turn on a flashlight, showing students the beam of light that is created. Next, turn the classroom lights on and shine the flashlight directly under an overhead light. Ask students if they can still see the beam of light from the flashlight. Guide students to realize that the flashlight is like a star. At night, when there is no light from the sun, we can see the stars shining brightly. However, during the day, the sun's light is so bright that we cannot see the stars, even though they are still there.

Earth & Space Science

MY ROCK REPORT

Name _____

20-Minute Science • ©The Mailbox® Books • TEC61363

- -

Take a Closer Look

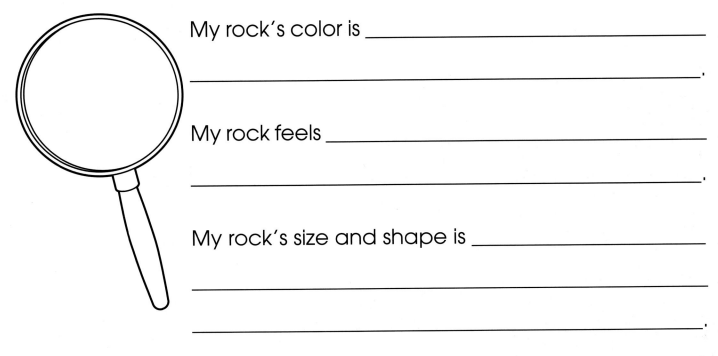

My rock's color is _____

_____.

My rock feels _____

_____.

My rock's size and shape is _____

_____.

1

Note to the teacher: Use with "Rock Report" on page 89.

Attractive Rocks

My rock _____ cling to a magnet.
(did or did not)

I learned _____

_____

_____.

2

Get Wet!

My rock _____.
(sinks or floats)

Note to the teacher: Use with "Rock Report" on page 89.

Nature Detectives
natural vs. man-made

Natural Items	Man-Made Items

Note to the teacher: Use with "Nature Detectives" on page 90.

Reduce, Reuse, and Recycle

by _____

20-Minute Science • ©The Mailbox® Books • TEC61363

Reduce

To reduce is to use less and create less waste.

1

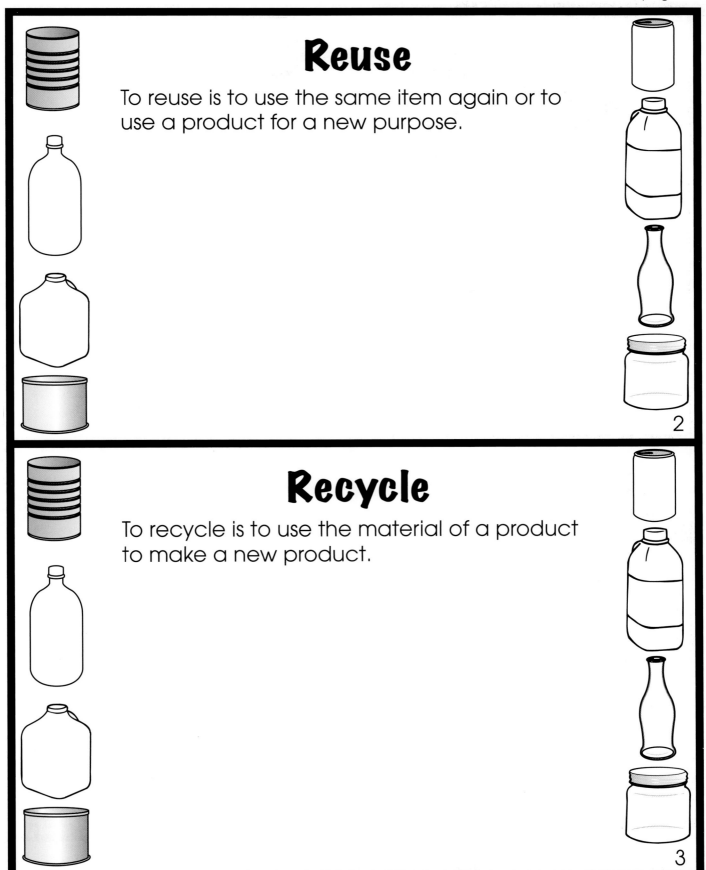

Reuse

To reuse is to use the same item again or to use a product for a new purpose.

2

Recycle

To recycle is to use the material of a product to make a new product.

3

Sun
and
Moon
Facts

Name _____

20-Minute Science • ©The Mailbox® Books • TEC61363

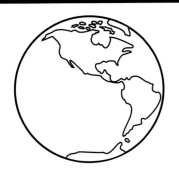

The _____

heats Earth.   **1**

The sun is a

_____.   **2**

The moon is made of rocks

and _____.   **3**

There is no

_____ on

the moon.   **4**

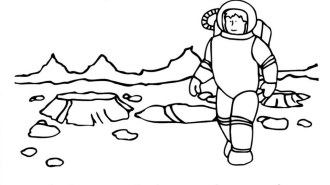

Astronauts have been to

the _____.   **5**

Word Bank
moon   star   dust   sun   air

Seasons

Dial-a-Season

Materials for each student:
9" white construction paper circle
9" yellow construction paper circle
yellow construction paper scraps
brad

Day 1: Discuss with students the characteristics of each season, such as weather, outdoor activities, and the changes in the appearance of trees. Then help each child fold her white circle in half twice to create four equal sections. Have each youngster illustrate (in sequential order) a different season in each section. Remind students to draw their illustrations facing the center of the circle as shown.

Day 2
Steps:
1. Review the seasons with youngsters.
2. Give students the following directions:
   —Fold the yellow circle in half twice to create four equal sections.
   —Cut one section from the circle.
   —Cut triangles (rays) from the yellow paper scraps.
   —Glue the triangles around the edge of the yellow circle.
3. Have each child place her yellow circle atop the illustrated circle. Help her secure them together in the center with a brad.
4. Encourage students to turn the wheel to see each of the four seasons.

Did You Know?
The changing seasons are caused by the changing position of the earth as it rotates around the sun.

Guess the Season

Help your students create these lift-the-flap booklets to review the seasons.

Materials for each student:
assembled copy of the booklet project on pages 104–106
patterns from the bottom of page 104

Steps:
1. Have each child write her name on her booklet cover.
2. Read the text on each booklet page and then have students glue on the flap of the corresponding pattern.
3. Suggest that students color their booklets. Then have youngsters use the booklets to review the unique characteristics of each season.

Earth & Space Science

Favorite Seasons

Materials:
graph like the one shown (without the cards)
class supply of blank cards

Display the graph. After reviewing the seasons with youngsters, assign each season a simple picture. Have each student draw on a card the picture that corresponds with his favorite season. Then invite each child, in turn, to share his favorite season and attach his card to the appropriate column on the graph.

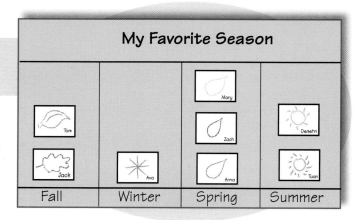

My Favorite Season

Fall	Winter	Spring	Summer
Tom / Jack	Ava	Mary / Zach / Anna	Demetri / Tuan

Seasonal Show-and-Tell

Materials:
seasonal objects

Give show-and-tell time a unique twist by inviting students to bring in seasonal items to share. Have each child bring one item to represent each season. As each child shares an item, have her classify it as a summer, fall, winter, or spring item. The have her explain how it relates to the specific season.

Fun for All Seasons

Materials for each student:
assembled banner project from page 107

Have each child draw a picture of his favorite thing to do in each season in the corresponding banner section. Then have him write (or dictate for you to write) to finish each sentence.

Earth & Space Science

Fall Changes

Materials for each student:
assembled copy of the booklet project on pages 108 and 109
tissue paper squares in fall colors

Steps:

1. Have each child write her name on her booklet cover.
2. Read the text on a booklet page and then give students the appropriate direction to follow.
   Page 1: Draw apples on the tree and in the basket.
   Page 2: Glue crumpled tissue paper squares on the leaf pile.
   Page 3: Draw a pile of acorns next to the squirrel.
3. Invite students to color their booklets; then encourage them to use their booklets to review the changes that take place in the fall.

Fall Poem

Materials:
class supply of page 110
large leaf cutout

Invite youngsters to brainstorm things they like to do in the fall and words that describe fall. List their ideas on the leaf cutout. Then give each child a copy of page 110 and have him fill in the blanks to complete the poem.

Earth & Space Science

Winter Wear

Materials for each student:
assembled copy of the booklet project on pages 111 and 112
copy of one set of patterns from page 113

Steps:
1. Have each child write his name on his booklet cover.
2. Read the text on a booklet page; then have each student glue a corresponding pattern on that page.
3. Continue for each booklet page.
4. Invite students to color their booklets.

Did You Know?
The first day of winter is the shortest day of the year.

Finding Food

Materials:
class supply of brown paper lunch sacks
supply of packing peanuts

While students are out of the room, scatter the packing peanuts around the classroom. Have students pretend they are wild animals and it is summer or fall. Then give each child a paper bag and invite her to gather as much food (packing peanuts) in her bag as she can. After about 20 seconds, invite students to return to their seats. Have each child count the number of peanuts she gathered and record the number on a piece of paper. Then have students pretend it is winter and take their empty bags and search for food. Upon returning to her seat, have each child count the number of peanuts she found in the winter and compare it to the number in her summer/fall collection. Lead students to understand that the food supply for wild animals greatly diminishes during the winter months, making it harder for them to find food.

Earth & Space Science

Signs of Spring

Materials for each student:
assembled copy of the booklet project on pages 115–117
copy of one set of patterns from page 114

Steps:
1. Have each child write his name on his booklet cover.
2. Read the text on a booklet page. Then direct each student to fold the corresponding pattern in half (except the sun) and glue it on the page where indicated.
3. Continue for each booklet page.
4. If desired, invite students to color their booklets.
5. Read the booklet with students, encouraging youngsters to lift each flap to reveal a different sign of spring.

Rules for Sun Safety
by Room 7

Wear sunglasses.

Don't stay out in the sun too long.

Always wear sunscreen, even if you're swimming.

If you feel burned, tell an adult.

The Hot Sun

Materials:
chart paper

Discuss with students how the sun can be helpful and also how it can be harmful. Then have youngsters brainstorm tips for being safe in the sun as you list their ideas on chart paper. Display the chart as a reminder to students about the importance of sun safety.

Shadow Hunting

Materials for each student:
piece of sidewalk chalk

On a sunny day, take students outside for a shadow hunt. Challenge each child to find a shadow being cast on the sidewalk or another paved area and trace its outline. Then, in turn, invite each child to share her outline with the class and identify the object that created it. For an added challenge, have classmates try to identify the object before it is revealed.

Sidewalk Chalk

Earth & Space Science

Guess the Season

Seasons come and seasons go.

How many seasons do you know?

Name _____

20-Minute Science • ©The Mailbox® Books • TEC61363

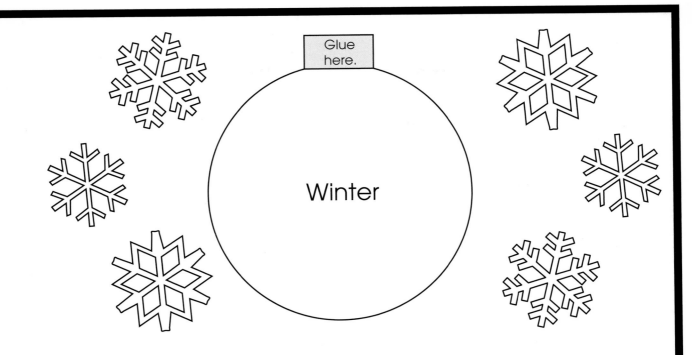

Shorter days and longer nights.
The color for this season is white, white, white.

1

Returning birds can be seen
As gentle rain makes things green.

2

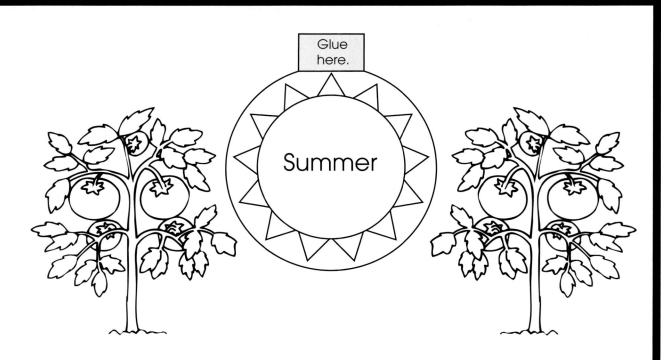

Tomatoes ripen on the vine
And days are filled with hot sunshine.

3

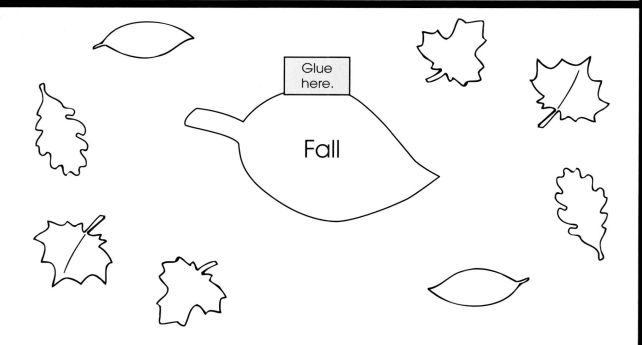

Leaves turn yellow, orange, and brown,
Then softly fall down, down, down.

4

Use with "Fun for All Seasons" on page 100.

Spring

In spring, I ______________________

____

______________________. 1

TEC61363

Name ______________________

Summer

In summer, I ______________________

____

______________________. 2

Fall

In fall, I ______________________

____

______________________. 3

Glue to page 2.

Winter

In winter, I ______________________

____

______________________. 4

Name _____

Fall Brings Changes for Us All

20-Minute Science • ©The Mailbox® Books • TEC61363

Farmers harvest many crops
and hope for days with a few raindrops.

1

People have to rake the leaves
and stay warm wearing longer sleeves.

2

Squirrels are gathering nuts and seeds.
They know where cooler weather leads.

3

Name _____

Fall Poem

Orange, yellow, red, and brown
Autumn leaves are falling down.

Squirrels are running all around,
Gathering nuts from the ground.

Pumpkins are growing on the vine.
It's cool and breezy—the weather's fine!

In the fall I like to _____

and _____

I think fall is _____

because _____

_____

_____

_____

_____

**Dressing
for
Winter**

by _____

20-Minute Science • ©The Mailbox® Books • TEC61363

I wear
a

1

I wear
warm

2

I wear
a

3

I wear
a

4

I wear
a

5

I wear

6

I am dressed
for winter!

7

Booklet Patterns

Use with "Signs of Spring" on page 103.

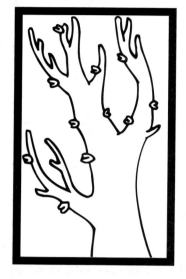

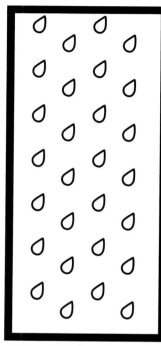

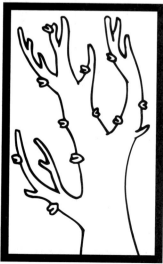

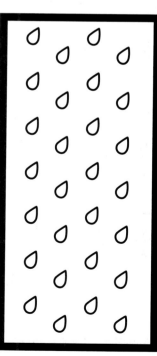

1

Glue sun here.

Warm sun shines.

Spring Is Here!

by _____

3

Glue flower here.

Flowers grow.

2

Glue rain here.

Rain falls.

20-Minute Science • ©The Mailbox® Books • TEC61363

5

Eggs hatch.

Glue birds here.

4

Buds open.

Glue branch here.

Weather

Snow, Rain, and Wind

Discuss with youngsters the similarities and differences between snowy, rainy, and windy weather. Then guide youngsters through the booklet project below.

Materials for each student:
copy of pages 124 and 125
two 5" x 7½" pieces of construction paper
blue ink pad
brad fastener

When it snows and I go out,
I wear my coat without a doubt.

Steps:
Day 1
1. Direct students to cut out the title label and glue it to a piece of construction paper to make the front cover of the booklet.
2. Read the text on a booklet page and then give students the appropriate direction to follow.

    Page 1: Color and cut out the coat. Glue the coat on the girl. Draw snowflakes around the girl.

    Page 2: Color and cut out the umbrella. Glue it on the page so it protects the boy from the rain. Make blue fingerprints (rain) around the boy.

    Page 3: Color and cut out the kite. Attach the bottom of the kite to the kite tail with a brad. Move the kite to show it waving in the breeze.
3. Have students set the pages aside.

Day 2
1. Review with students the characteristics of rainy, snowy, and windy weather.
2. Direct students to cut out their booklet pages.
3. Have each student stack his pages in order between the prepared front cover and the remaining piece of construction paper.
4. Encourage students to color their booklets and use them to review different types of weather.

Earth & Space Science

Rain Gauge

Have students use these completed rain gauges to track the rainfall near their homes.

Materials for each student:
2-liter bottle with top removed and edges taped
clay
ruler
permanent marker

Steps for students:
1. Place a flat layer of clay in the bottom of the bottle.
2. Use the ruler and marker to draw one-inch increments on the outside of the bottle, beginning one inch above the layer of clay as shown. (Provide help as needed.)
3. Place the rain gauge outside in an open area.

Wonderful Windsock

Encourage youngsters to hang these completed projects outside to see which direction the wind is blowing.

Materials for each student:
12" x 18" sheet of laminated construction paper, stapled into a cylinder
2" x 16" laminated tagboard strip
length of twine
lengths of ribbon or yarn

Help each student staple her ribbon or yarn lengths to the inside bottom edge of her cylinder. Then assist her in stapling the tagboard strip to the top of the cylinder to make a handle. Help her tie the twine around the handle. Then invite each child to take her windsock home and suspend it outside where it can move about freely.

Did You Know?
Wind is caused by the uneven heating of the earth's surface. The air above warm spots on the surface also becomes warmer. As warm air rises, cool air is sucked under the warm air to take its place. This air motion causes wind.

Earth & Space Science

Weather Watcher

Materials:
laminated copy of page 126
silly sunglasses (weather-watching glasses)
weather-related pointer (dowel with a large laminated sun
    or raindrop cutout attached)
dry-erase marker

Choose a volunteer to be the weather watcher for the day. Have the child put on the sunglasses as you assist him in observing the weather. Help the student record the information on the chart. Then invite him to use the pointer to share the data with the class. Erase the chart at the end of the day to ready it for your next weather watcher.

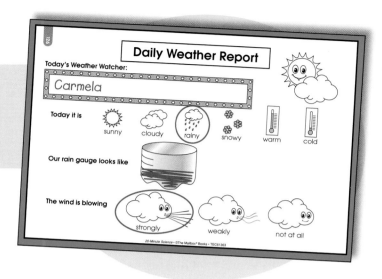

Rain	
☺	☹

helps flowers grow
waters our garden
gives water to
    animals
makes puddles to
    play in
	makes the lawn
	    messy
	we can't play
	    outside
	can cause floods
	makes it muddy in
	    the yard

Rain—Go Away or Stay?

Materials:
chart labeled with the headings shown

Ask students to share positive and negative things about rain as you record each response in the appropriate chart column. Display the chart to remind students that, at times, they might want rain to go away but sometimes it is better for the rain to stay!

Earth & Space Science

A Stormy Song

Have students brainstorm types of severe weather as you list their ideas on the board. Then lead them in singing this toe-tapping tune.

(sung to the tune of "If You're Happy and You Know It")

Thunderstorms have rain and then a flash. Boom! Crash!
Thunderstorms have rain and then a flash. Boom! Crash!
All that thunder with its noise
Wakes up little girls and boys.
Thunderstorms have rain and then a flash. Boom! Crash!

Tornadoes have a lot of swirling wind. Whoosh! Swoosh!
Tornadoes have a lot of swirling wind. Whoosh! Swoosh!
To the basement we shall go,
Where we'll miss this windy show!
Tornadoes have a lot of swirling wind. Whoosh! Swoosh!

Hurricanes come blowing from the sea. Whoo-eee!
Hurricanes come blowing from the sea. Whoo-eee!
All the wind and waves look grim—
Not a good day for a swim!
Hurricanes come blowing from the sea. Whoo-eee!

Our Forecast				
Day	Forecast	What should we wear?	Can we go outside?	Was the forecast correct?
Monday	☀			
Tuesday				
Wednesday				
Thursday				
Friday				

Be Prepared!

Materials:
chart similar to the one shown
weather forecast for at least the next 5 days

Display the weather forecast and the chart. Discuss the forecast for the current day as you record it on the chart. Then ask students the next two questions on the chart and record their responses. At the end of the school day, have students help you fill out the last column on the chart. Begin the next day with a review of the previous day's information. At the end of the week, lead students in discussing why it is important to know the weather forecast and how a weather forecast helps prepare them for both calm and dangerous weather.

Earth & Space Science

Sequence of a Storm

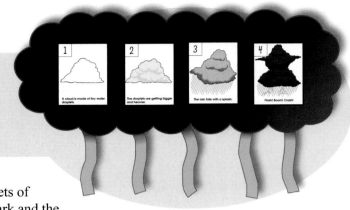

Materials:
class supply of page 127
class supply of 12" x 18" black construction paper
blue tissue paper strips
shallow container of water
several sponges cut into cloud shapes

Day 1

Explain to students that clouds are made of tiny droplets of water. When the droplets get too heavy, the clouds turn dark and the water falls to the earth as rain. Place the sponges in the container of water. Allow several children at a time to explore how the sponges hold a certain amount of water before drops begin to fall back into the container.

Day 2
Steps:

1. Have students cut a large cloud shape from the construction paper.
2. Then direct youngsters to cut out the cards.
3. Read the text on each card and have each child arrange his cards in order.
4. Have youngsters number each card 1–4 and glue the cards in order on the cloud.
5. Direct students to glue tissue paper strips to the bottom of the cloud so they represent rain.

Hurricane Hazards

Share the poem shown with students and discuss the possible wind and water damage that can be caused by a hurricane. Then lead students through the steps to complete the project.

Mr. Hurricane
When old Mr. Hurricane blows in from the sea,
He seems just as angry as he could be!
The waves pound the shore with a smack, smack, smack.
And the rain hits the house with a crack, crack, crack!
He picks things up and he blows things down,
When old Mr. Hurricane comes to town!

Materials for each student:
copy of page 128 with a slit cut along the
    dotted line in the water
black tissue paper scraps
blue construction paper scrap

Steps:

1. Color and cut out the pictures at the bottom of the page.
2. Glue them where indicated.
3. Crumple black tissue paper scraps and glue them to the clouds at the top of the page so they look like storm clouds.
4. Cut a wave shape from the blue paper and insert it in the slit as shown.
5. Move the wave shape up and down and lift the flaps to view the wind damage that can be caused by a hurricane.

Earth & Space Science

Twister!

Explain to students that a tornado is a storm of swirling wind that acts like a vacuum cleaner. When a tornado touches the ground, it sucks up objects and debris in its path.

Materials for each student:
12" x 18" white construction paper
brown fingerpaint
natural items, such as leaves, twigs, and pebbles

Steps for students:
1. Place a small amount of fingerpaint on the paper.
2. Swirl the paint to create the funnel of a tornado.
3. Glue the natural items onto the tornado to represent debris the tornado has sucked up from the ground.

Lightning Bolt

Talk with students about what lightning is and what it does. Then place a thin layer of black and purple paint in a shallow pan. Finally, guide students through the steps to create a cloud-to-ground lightning picture.

Materials for each student:
12" x 18" white construction paper
9" x 12" black construction paper
1"-wide yellow construction paper strips
paper towel

Steps for students:
1. Crumple the paper towel and dip it in the paint.
2. Press the paper towel repeatedly on the white paper.
3. Repeat as desired.
4. Cut a cloud shape from the black paper. When the paint is dry, glue the cloud to the paper.
5. Rip or cut the yellow construction paper strips into separate lengths.
6. Glue the lengths onto the painting so they resemble a lightning bolt.

Did You Know?
Lightning can leap from one cloud to another or from a cloud to the ground.

Earth & Space Science

Weather Is All Around Us!

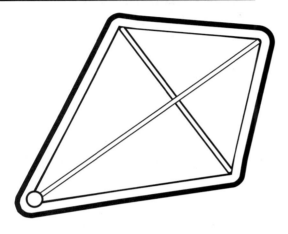

When it snows and I go out,
I wear my coat without a doubt.

20-Minute Science • ©The Mailbox® Books • TEC61363

1

When the rain comes down in drops,
Up, up, up my umbrella pops!

2

On a very windy day,
My kite will twist, bend, and sway.

3

Daily Weather Report

Today's Weather Watcher:

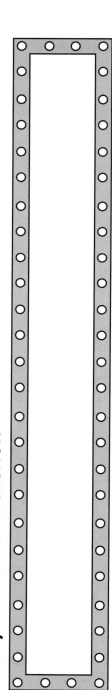

cold

warm

Today it is

 sunny

 cloudy

 rainy

 snowy

Our rain gauge looks like

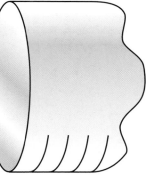

The wind is blowing

 not at all

 weakly

 strongly

20-Minute Science • ©The Mailbox® Books • TEC61363

Note to the teacher: Use with "Weather Watcher" on page 120.

TEC61363

The rain falls with a splash.

Flash! Boom! Crash!

The droplets are getting bigger and heavier.

A cloud is made of tiny water droplets.

Hurricane Hazards

Listen and do.

20-Minute Science • ©The Mailbox® Books • TEC61363

Note to the teacher: Use with "Hurricane Hazards" on page 122.